WILLIAM COOPER is an attorney, national columnist, and award-winning author. His commentary has appeared in hundreds of publications around the world, including the *New York Times*, *Washington Post*, *CNN*, *San Francisco Chronicle*, *Chicago Sun-Times*, *Dallas Morning News*, *Huffington Post*, *Toronto Star*, and *Jerusalem Post*. *Publishers Weekly* calls his writings about American politics "a compelling rallying cry for democratic institutions under threat in America."

Visit him online at Will-Cooper.com

T0019564

Also by William Cooper

Non-fiction
Stress Test

Fiction
A Quiet Life

HOW AMERICA WORKS ...

A Brief Guide to the
US Political System

AND WHY IT DOESN'T

William Cooper

First published in the UK in 2024 by Gemini Adult Books Ltd,
part of the Gemini Books Group

Based in Woodbridge and London

Marine House, Tide Mill Way,
Woodbridge, Suffolk IP12 1AP

www.geminibooks.com

Paperback ISBN 9781802472066
eBook ISBN 9781802472431

A CIP catalogue record for this book is available from
the British Library.

Every reasonable effort has been made to trace copyright-holders of
material reproduced in this book, but if any have been inadvertently
overlooked the publishers would be glad to hear from them.

Printed in the UK
10 9 8 7 6 5 4 3 2 1

To my family.

Praise for William Cooper's Writing

"William Cooper has seen the future, and it is—or can be—a lot better than our recent past. Reading *How America Works … And Why It Doesn't* and inhaling his wisdom is taking a resolute step toward a better democracy for us all."

Michael McKinley, bestselling author of *Yardley's Ace: Making and Breaking American Military Intelligence*

"A compelling and sensible overview of America's emerging democratic crisis … [*Stress Test's*] reasoned tone and bipartisan critiques are a welcome perspective in an increasingly polarized and heated political landscape."

Kirkus Reviews

"*Stress Test* is a compelling rallying cry for democratic institutions under threat in America [and] perfect for readers eager for a non-partisan analysis of the threat to American democracy"

Publishers Weekly

"William Cooper is an insightful and thought-provoking writer about US politics. He deserves to be widely read."

Thomas Plate, Editorial Page Editor (former), *Los Angeles Times*

William Cooper's writing is "such a great tool for classrooms or for any place where people would like to have a civil conversation about things"

Robin Colucci, host of *Authors' Corner*

"William Cooper is one of the most insightful writers covering politics in America today. It has been a privilege to have him as a guest on my podcast and I am grateful someone like William is chronicling these volatile times."

Erik R. Fleming, host of the award-winning
podcast *A Moment with Erik Fleming*

"Prodigious"

The Tennessean

"Contrarian"

Jacobin

"Thought-provoking"

Skiatook Journal

"Very insightful"

The City Paper, Bogotá

"A welcome splash of reality on money, law and politics"
Tennessee Tribune

"William Cooper presents an insightful, sensitive, and accessible account of the trials that face American democracy in the twenty-first century. This fair- and broad-minded volume makes compelling reading for those who are looking to build a better democracy."

Alexander Yen, University of Oxford

"Partisanship fuels personal convictions more than ever in our society, and convictions fuel mysided thinking and other cognitive biases. At no time have we needed this discussion of bias and partisan thinking more than now."

Keith E. Stanovich, author of *The Bias That Divides Us*

CONTENTS

CONTENTS

"The truth unquestionably is, that the only path to a subversion of the republican system of the country is, by flattering the prejudices of the people, and exciting their jealousies and apprehensions, to throw affairs into confusion, and bring on civil commotion"

Alexander Hamilton (1792)

"There are only two industries that call their customers 'users': illegal drugs and software"

Edward Tufte (1995)

Preface

A frenzy of polarization and misgovernance has engulfed American politics. Actors and institutions—on both sides of the political divide—are silencing disfavored speech. Prosecutors around the country are criminalizing politics. The Republican party is openly sabotaging the electoral system. And a new breed of social-media celebrities in Congress is failing to address myriad public-policy failures, from a broken immigration system to hugely expensive and dysfunctional healthcare to staggering economic inequality. These problems have powerful momentum behind them—and will likely persist far into the future.

All around the world people are asking: *What's wrong with America? Why isn't it working?*

The answer isn't one of the common partisan narratives. It isn't the "radical progressives" who want to tear the system down. Nor is it the "deplorable conservatives" who want to punish America's elites. It's not a dysfunctional, gridlocked Congress. Nor is it a right-wing, reactionary Supreme Court.

It's not an aging Joe Biden. Nor is it an ever-angrier Donald Trump (though he sure isn't helping).

The answer, rather, is broader than any narrow category or single person. The answer is the American people themselves. A nation is, above all, the hearts and minds of its people. And Americans in the twenty-first century are becoming increasingly untethered from both reality and the essential principles and traditions that have shaped their nation's historic success. A big part of why America isn't working is because far too many Americans neither know nor care how it's supposed to work.

The root cause of this mania is the combination of three deeply connected things. The first is tribalism. Americans, like all humans, have deep tribal roots. This expresses itself in powerful biases in favor of one's own political clan— and searing antipathy for the other side. The second is social media. Sophisticated algorithms behind major online platforms exploit Americans' cognitive vulnerabilities and intensify their tribal prejudices. And the third is the structure of the US political system itself. The two-party system amplifies and exacerbates polarization by pitting two juggernauts (Democrats and Republicans) against each other in a bitter, all-consuming rivalry—and gerrymandering, closed primaries, and the Electoral College compound the problem.

This flywheel spins faster every day. And it's culminating in two overlapping threats to the American experiment. The first is the criminalization of politics, as prosecutors from around the country set their sights on partisan rivals. Since every political salvo must be met with greater opposite force, this has set in motion a pernicious dynamic that is spiraling into catastrophe. The second threat involves the central premise of American government: the sanctity of the vote. America's election system is under attack. And not just by ineffectual zealots at the margins of power or howling mobs in the street, but by the Republican party's undisputed leader, Donald Trump, and his loyalists throughout federal and state government.

This book has two parts. Part One (Chapters 1–5) explains how America works. Chapter 1 places the American experiment into historical context. Chapter 2 tells the story of the United States Constitution—its background, construction, and reasoning. Chapter 3 focuses on the worst provisions in the Constitution—which protected slavery and still protect guns—and traces their impact throughout American history. Chapter 4 turns to the essential Constitutional principles that have shaped America for the better: separation of powers, federalism, and free speech. Chapter 5 analyzes essential traditions that aren't in the Constitution but are nonetheless central to the American story: the two-party political system, the rule of law, and capitalism.

Part Two (Chapters 6–10) explains why America isn't working. Chapter 6 examines the root cause of Americans' irrationality: the combination of tribalism, social media, and structural defects in the political system. Chapter 7 homes in on the political dysfunction that this combination produces. Chapter 8 walks through numerous public-policy failures that America's gridlocked government fails to address. Chapter 9 warns of the two biggest threats to American democracy:

criminalizing politics and undermining election integrity. Finally, Chapter 10 looks ahead and assesses America's role in the world in the future.

Twenty-first-century America isn't working the way it's supposed to. This book explains why.

PART ONE

HOW AMERICA WORKS

"Freedom is nothing but a chance to be better"
Albert Camus

1

History

"History, in general, only informs us what bad government is"
Thomas Jefferson

To understand America you must first understand human history. Building and sustaining a government that broadly promotes human flourishing is hard—and until recently most attempts to do so had failed. When America's founders wrote its Constitution in 1787, the history of government had been long, dark, and harsh.

For starters, most nations were dominated by kings and tyrants. A small, elite class typically controlled all the wealth and resources. While the great majority labored in hardship and difficulty. This reality caused James Madison, America's fourth president, to worry that history's iron law of kings dominating governments would ensnare the new nation: "We have heard of the impious doctrine in the old world, that the people were made for kings, not kings for the people. Is the same doctrine to be revived in the new, in another shape ...?"

Second, wars and conquest—perpetrated by these kings—were common. Between 1492 (when Spanish explorer Christopher Columbus landed in the Bahamas) and 1787, violent wars took a brutal toll on humanity.[1] To name a few: the Thirty Years' War in Europe; the Qing conquest of the Ming in Asia; the Manchu conquest of China; the Spanish conquest of South America; and the Seven Years' War across the globe. According to Oxford University's *Our World in Data*, the per capita death rate from wars during this period was exponentially higher than it is today.[2]

Third, government-sanctioned slavery was ubiquitous. As Brown University's *Report on Slavery and Justice* explains,[3] humans owning humans was etched into the fabric of civilization. "The oldest surviving system of written laws, the Code of Hammurabi, includes regulations about slavery, as does the Old Testament. Slavery was ubiquitous in the classical world; about a third of the inhabitants of ancient Athens were slaves, roughly the same proportion as in the antebellum American South. Slavery existed in the Muslim world (usually as a status reserved for non-Muslims) and in Mesoamerica, in Africa and Asia, and in western and eastern Europe." One prominent example of slavery was the Transatlantic Slave Trade, which began in the fifteenth century. Over several centuries more than 12 million Africans were forcibly transported in European ships to the Americas as slaves.[4]

Finally, governments consistently failed to protect their people from nature's dangers, such as disease, famine, and harsh weather. The "Great Frost" of 1740, for example, was a severely cold winter that devastated countries throughout

Europe. The average lifespan globally in 1800 was between 26 and 35 years, depending on the geographical location.[5]

This is not to say that governmental failure made every dimension of human history grim. By 1787, human accomplishments in the arts and sciences were modest yet impressive. And plenty of people had led good lives, particularly those fortunate enough not to toil in servitude. Nor is it true that every constituted government had been an abject failure from the outset. Before its fall, Ancient Rome, for example, was one of the first examples of representative democracy in the world.[6]

But these were the exceptions—not the rule. And despite the common tendency to romanticize history, English political philosopher Thomas Hobbes (1588–1679) aptly described human life in his time as "nasty, brutish, and short." As economic historian Nathan Rosenberg clarifies: "The eras of misery [before America's founding] have been mythologized and may even be remembered as golden ages of pastoral simplicity. They were not."

As we'll see in Part Two, today this history is lost on many Americans, who exuberantly critique the country on a blank slate. Void of context, these critics rail against America for its past sins and present defects—of which there are many to highlight. Famed intellectual Noam Chomsky, for example, has even condemned America as a "failed state." According to Chomsky in 2020, "Fifteen years ago, I wrote a book called *Failed States* ... referring to states that are incapable of meeting the needs of citizens, in the most important case because of deep policy choices, and are a danger not only to their own citizens but the world.

The prime example was the United States … I still stand by that judgment…"

There's little utility in this pastime, at least if the desire to be accurate is present. Focusing only on America's sins—or judging it only against utopias that never existed—is grossly misleading. The analysis must be put in context. Evaluating America must be anchored in the stark realities of human history.

AMERICA'S FOUNDING

America's founders understood this history. And the founders' experiment in self-governance was specifically engineered to address its horrors. To do so, they turned to the principles and sensibilities of the Enlightenment, the seventeenth- and eighteenth-century intellectual movement in Europe that emphasized reason and science instead of religious dogmatism and blind faith.

Most of the founders' ideas for America weren't new. The founders weren't great innovators; they were, instead, brilliant implementers. As Thomas Jefferson, America's third president, explained in a letter nearly fifty years after he drafted the Declaration of Independence:

> This was the object of the Declaration of Independence. Not to find out new principles, or new arguments, never before thought of, not merely to say things which had never been said before, but to place before mankind the common sense of the subject, in terms so plain and firm as to command their assent, and to justify ourselves in the independent stand we are compelled to take. Neither aiming at originality of

principle or sentiment, not yet copied from any particular and previous writing, it was intended to be an expression of the American mind, and to give to that expression the proper tone and spirit called for by the occasion. All it's [sic] authority rests on the harmonizing sentiments of the day, whether expressed in conversation, letters, printed essays, or in the elementary books of public right, as Aristotle, Cicero, Locke, Sidney, & c.

Jefferson highlighted several intellectuals who influenced America's founding and design. The first is Aristotle, the ancient Greek philosopher. Aristotle recognized that human freedom was the central concern of democratic government: "The basic premise of the democratic sort of regime is freedom." And he understood that to achieve freedom and equality, government authority must reside in the people broadly and not narrowly in kings and despots: "For, if liberty and equality, as some persons suppose, are chiefly to be found in a democracy, they will be attained when all persons alike share in the government to the utmost."

Jefferson also cites Cicero, a leading statesman, orator, and writer during the late Roman republic. Cicero understood the dangers inherent in concentrated governmental power: "When a government becomes powerful it is destructive, extravagant and violent; it is an usurer which takes bread from innocent mouths and deprives honorable men of their substance, for votes with which to perpetuate itself." This deep fear of government power pervades America's Constitutional framework

John Locke was another of Jefferson's inspirations. Locke was a seventeenth-century British political philosopher and medical researcher. He emphasized the inherent connection between individual freedom, government by consent, and majoritarian rule. "Men being, as has been said, by nature, all free, equal, and independent," Locke wrote in his *Second Treatise on Civil Government*, "no one can be put out of this estate, and subjected to the political power of another, without his own consent." Moreover, Locke continued, "the only way whereby any one divests himself of his natural liberty, and puts on the bonds of civil society, is by agreeing with other men to join and unite into a community for their comfortable, safe, and peaceable living one amongst another ..."

Finally, Jefferson references Algernon Sidney, an Englishman executed by the government in 1683 for allegedly trying to assassinate King Charles II. Sidney's *Discourses Concerning Government* and other writings inspired revolutionaries in America and elsewhere. He despised despots: "I will believe in the right of one man to govern a nation despotically when I find a man born unto the world with boots and spurs, and a nation with saddles on their backs." And he was fearless and outspoken in his quest for freedom: "If his Majesty is resolved to have my head, he may make a whistle of my arse if he pleases." A zealous hatred for despots fueled America's revolution and underpins its basic government structure.

These and other pro-democracy intellectuals were well known in 1787. Until that time, however, kings had won the battle between tyranny and democracy. Madison's "impious doctrine" reigned: people had been "made for kings." Not the other way around. America was an experiment bent on destroying that order—on vanquishing the throne—and putting the ideals of democracy and self-governance into practice.

2

The Constitution

"[W]hatever fine declarations may be inserted in any Constitution [it] must altogether depend on public opinion, and on the general spirit of the people and of the government"
Alexander Hamilton

The primary mechanism for pursuing this goal was a written Constitution. America's Constitutional Convention occurred in 1787, several years after the Revolutionary War. In addition to addressing the errors that long plagued history's governments, the founders sought to correct the recent defects of the Articles of Confederation.[7]

There were many. The Articles outlined the alliance between America's several states. The arrangement was, to put it charitably, a train wreck. The central government was weak and dysfunctional, lacking both executive and judicial functions. The legislature couldn't levy taxes to fund its operations and relied instead on voluntary state payments. The states had their own currencies, stifling trade among them. And after the war, the new nation's economy was so weak it couldn't settle its substantial war debts to European countries and investors.

Shays' Rebellion[8] in 1786 and 1787 brought the Confederation's embarrassing weakness into stark relief. The central government couldn't even quell a small tax protest by Western Massachusetts farmers. Led by Daniel Shays, a former revolutionary soldier, the rebellion initially was confined to several violent attacks on government buildings. It ballooned into a full-scale military confrontation before finally—months later—being subdued.

Today many Americans on the right glorify this post-war era as the triumphant celebration of a blossoming young democracy. Not quite. The nebulous alliance between the states hung together by the thinnest of threads, barely surviving each successive day. Mistakes, blunders, and setbacks dominated the fledging government. And everything could easily have been different: a negative twist here, an unfortunate turn there, and the American experiment could have died in the womb. America's Constitution was thus inspired as much by the stress of the young nation's post-war crisis as by the energy of the founders' political passions.

The Constitution was a carefully engineered response to the enormous challenges—old and new, grand and practical—inherent in forming a lasting and effective government. It was enacted on June 21, 1788, when New Hampshire became the ninth state to ratify it. The drafters set forth their goals in the Preamble: "We the people of the United States, in order to form a more perfect union, establish justice, insure domestic tranquility, provide for the common defense, promote the general welfare, and secure the blessings of liberty to ourselves and our posterity, do ordain and establish this Constitution for the United States of America."

Merely 4,400 words, the Constitution[9] has seven articles that form the basic structure of American government:

- Article I outlines the Legislative Branch, including Congress's power to pass legislation, borrow money, and declare war.
- Article II outlines the Executive Branch, including the President's power to enter treaties, nominate federal judges, and command the military.
- Article III outlines the Judicial Branch, including judges' power to rule on "cases and controversies" between litigants.
- Article IV outlines the responsibilities of the federal government and state governments.
- Article V outlines the Constitutional-amendment process.
- Article VI declares the assumption of the Confederation's debts, asserts the pre-eminence of federal law, and requires government officials to swear an oath to the Constitution.
- Article VII states that the ratification of nine states shall be sufficient to enact the Constitution.

A vital source for understanding how America works, the Federalist Papers emerged shortly after Americans ratified the Constitution. The Federalist Papers were a series of eighty-five newspaper columns written by political leaders James Madison, Alexander Hamilton, and John Jay under the pen name Publius. The columns expounded on the new Constitution's reasoning, language, and structure.

For example, Hamilton, in Federalist 22, echoed John Locke in highlighting the central importance of government by consent: "The fabric of American empire ought to rest on the solid basis of *the consent of the people*. The streams of national power ought to flow immediately from that pure, original fountain of all legitimate authority." (Author's emphasis.)

Madison, in Federalist 51, explained how the structure of government must be designed to accept and harness the realities of human nature: "If men were angels, no government would be necessary. If angels were to govern men, neither external nor internal controls on government would be necessary. In framing a government which is to be administered by men over men, the great difficulty lies in this: you must first enable the government to control the governed; and in the next place oblige it to control itself." And Madison, in Federalist 48, emphasized the vital importance of governmental checks and balances: "An elective despotism was not the government we fought for; but one ... in which the powers of government should be so divided and balanced among several bodies of magistracy, as that no one could transcend their legal limits, without being effectually checked and restrained by the others."

Today, many critics focus myopically on the Constitution's errors. Columnist Ryan Cooper, for example, shares sentiments with many on the left: "The American Constitution is an outdated, malfunctioning piece of junk— and it's only getting worse. When written, the Constitution made a morally hideous compromise with slavery that took a war and 750,000 lives to make right. And while its basic structure sort of worked for awhile in the 20th century, the

Constitution is now falling prey to the same defects that [have] toppled every other similar governing document the world over."

Meanwhile, many triumphalists over-emphasize the Constitution's virtues. America's 40th president, Ronald Reagan (still a conservative champion), expressed sentiments common on the right: "If our Constitution has endured, through times perilous as well as prosperous, it has not been simply as a plan of government, no matter how ingenious or inspired that might be. This document that we honor today has always been something more to us, filled us with a deeper feeling than one of simple admiration—a feeling, one might say, more of reverence."

Neither extreme is correct. Some parts of the Constitution are, in fact, quite dreadful. And some parts are, unquestionably, extremely positive. America's founding document should thus be condemned *and* celebrated—not one or the other. It is indeed a great irony of human history that the same document that contains numerous searing abominations—some of which still reverberate today—also sets forth an essential architecture of government that has dramatically increased human flourishing.

3

Constitutional Abominations

"He must be able to detect no inconsistencies in slavery;
he must be made to feel that slavery is right; and he can be
brought to that only when he ceases to be a man"
Frederick Douglass

THREE-FIFTHS AND SLAVE-TRADE CLAUSES

Several Constitutional provisions have fundamentally shaped the American experience. Let's start with the abominations. The first and most notorious is the Three-Fifths Clause. This provision awarded states an additional three-fifths of a person for every slave when counting the population to determine Congressional representation: "Representatives and direct Taxes shall be apportioned among the several States which may be included within this Union, according to their respective Numbers, which shall be determined by adding to the whole Number of free Persons, including those bound to Service for a Term of Years, and excluding Indians not taxed, three fifths of all other Persons [i.e., slaves]."

Slave-holding states thus received a great reward for their terrible sin: an outsized influence in Congress. And because the Constitution's Electoral College appoints states' electors based on Congressional representation, slave-holding states also got a leg up with presidential elections. The Three-Fifths Clause may even have handed Virginia's Thomas Jefferson (a major slaveholder himself) the presidency in 1800.[10] Indeed, the Three-Fifths Clause didn't just protect slavery; it dramatically incentivized the practice: the more slaves southern states acquired, the more government power they amassed.

The Three-Fifths Clause wasn't the only provision emblazing slavery into America's founding document. The founders also included the Slave-Trade Clause. This Constitutional requirement was chilling: no prohibition could be placed on the fundamental right of Americans to import slaves into the country for twenty years: "The Migration or Importation of such Persons [i.e., slaves] as any of the States now existing shall think proper to admit, shall not be prohibited by the Congress prior to the Year one thousand eight hundred and eight, but a Tax or duty may be imposed on such Importation, not exceeding ten dollars for each Person."

Unlike many other topics important to the nascent country, the slave trade was so critical to the founders that they enshrined it in the Constitution. In the eighty years that followed, the importation of slaves cast a dark and bloody shadow over the emerging nation.

Both of these Constitutional provisions are a vile stain on America's past. One of human history's worst practices was not just prevalent in America, was not just condoned, was not just encouraged, but was so essential that the founders gave it protections and advantages in the nation's founding document and highest law. It ultimately took a civil war to end slavery in America. And in the war's aftermath, three Constitutional amendments addressed the subject:

- The 13th Amendment abolished slavery unless it resulted from conviction for a crime: "Section 1: Neither slavery nor involuntary servitude, except as a punishment for crime whereof the party shall have been duly convicted, shall exist within the United States, or any place subject to their jurisdiction."
- The 14th Amendment made former slaves and their lineage United States citizens and thereby entitled to the rights and protections afforded by citizenship: "Section 1: All persons born or naturalized in the United States, and subject to the jurisdiction thereof, are citizens of the United States and of the State wherein they reside."
- The 15th Amendment granted former slaves the right to vote and prohibited limiting the franchise because of race: "Section 1: The right of citizens of the United States to vote shall not be denied or abridged by the United States or by any State on account of race, color, or previous condition of servitude."

Enacting these amendments was a necessary and important step in atoning for the past. And America has consistently broadened the rights and protections of its citizens. Still, the Civil-War amendments do not lessen, let alone erase, all the horror that preceded them. And post-Civil-War Reconstruction was blighted by racial atrocities, as southern states resisted the amendments' dictates. Indeed, white racists consistently perpetrated horrific, gratuitous crimes against Black people well into the twentieth century.

During the 1921 Tulsa Race Massacre, for example, a white mob destroyed the predominantly Black Greenwood neighborhood in Tulsa, Oklahoma. Hundreds of people were killed and thousands left homeless. Yet at the time of the massacre, news reports were largely suppressed, and few Americans knew about this atrocity for nearly a century.

Several decades later, on August 28, 1955, a Black child from Chicago named Emmett Till was brutally murdered in Money, Mississippi. He allegedly flirted with a white woman. The murderers were the woman's husband and his brother. They ordered Emmett to carry a 75-pound cotton gin fan to the Tallahatchie River and forced him to take off his clothes. Then they beat him, gouged out his eye, and shot him in the head. Then they tied his body to the cotton gin fan with barbed wire and threw it into the river.

Moreover, Jim Crow—the system of express legal discrimination against Black people—long prevailed in the American South. Named after a Black minstrel show character, Jim Crow lasted a century—from the post-Civil-War era until the 1968 Civil Rights Act. The legal system denied Black people numerous fundamental rights, including the right to vote, to hold a job, and to get an education. Those who dared to violate Jim Crow's laws (or who were merely accused of doing so) were often arrested, fined, imprisoned, and even murdered.

The wounds from this recent history are still fresh. Tensions are still high. And race is still "the fault line in American politics," according to Barack Obama, America's first Black president. Recent trends are disappointing. A July 2021 Gallup poll reveals that "U.S. adults' positive ratings of relations between Black and White Americans are at their lowest point in more than two decades of measurement. Currently, 42% of Americans say relations between the two groups are 'very' or 'somewhat' good, while 57% say they are 'somewhat' or 'very' bad."

Two momentous factors contribute to this recent nadir in race relations. The first is Obama's presidency. While in hindsight many forget his long odds, Obama's victories in both 2008 and 2012 were shocking triumphs in American history: a nation deeply scarred by its abuse of Black people elected a Black man as its head of state. Twice. The second factor is the reaction to Obama—and his name is Donald J. Trump. Obama's presidency deeply unsettled and angered millions of Americans not ready for a Black president. And Trump's hostility to minorities (sometimes subtle, sometimes overt, always cunning) drives his popularity among many Republicans, particularly in southern states.

Some commentators think little has changed since before the Civil War. Michelle Alexander, author of *The New Jim Crow: Mass Incarceration in the Age of Colorblindness*, for example, puts it this way: "We have not ended racial caste in America; we have merely redesigned it ... Indeed, a primary function of any racial caste system is to define the meaning of race in its time. Slavery defined what it meant to be black (a slave), and Jim Crow defined what it meant to be black (a second-class citizen). Today mass incarceration defines the meaning of blackness in America: black people, especially black men, are criminals. That is what it means to be black."

Others downplay and rationalize slavery's central role in America's past. Republican Senator from Arkansas Tom Cotton, for example, called slavery a "necessary evil": "We have to study the history of slavery and its role and impact on the development of our country because otherwise we can't understand our country. As the founding fathers said, it was the necessary evil upon which the union was built, but the union was built in a way, as Lincoln said, to put slavery on the course to its ultimate extinction."

Both versions are far too simple. American slavery was every bit as horrific as the harshest critics assert. Allowing slavery wasn't necessary—it was a *choice* the founders *elected* to make. And there are no excuses, countervailing considerations, or subsequent redemptions that soften America's profound culpability.

Yet this stain does not permeate and define every dimension of America and its history. Neither persons nor nations should be categorically defined by their worst acts, especially when their best acts have been highly consequential. And while mass incarceration is a truly abhorrent American failure (see Chapter 8), race relations in America have improved since before the Civil War ended slavery—obviously—and have not been "merely redesigned."

America's history of slavery and racism doesn't nullify its achievements promoting the arts, furthering the sciences, and, yes, fundamentally expanding the realm of human freedom. America's original sin isn't justified by its subsequent contributions to human flourishing; but neither does that sin render those contributions void. Rather, the positive and negative elements of America's past all coexist together—the whole damn thing—in bitter and uncomfortable contradiction, irony, pain, and truth.

VOTING RIGHTS

The founders left the right to vote—i.e., to participate in American democracy—to the states, who were Constitutionally empowered to select "the times, places and manner of holding elections for Senators and Representatives," while Congress was given the power to "make or alter such regulations." Thus, instead of building rules for elections into the Constitution, America's elites empowered themselves to subsequently choose who voted and who didn't. The result was predictable: the very class of people who drafted and ratified the Constitution—property-owning white men—were the only people given the franchise. Missing were women, people of color, and poor white men.

It wasn't until after the Civil War that Black men could vote. And it wasn't until the 19th Amendment in 1920—132 years after the founding!—that American women achieved this basic civic right. What the founders left out of the Constitution was thus just as impactful as what they put in. The hypocrisy was searing: a nation founded on the revolutionary idea that "all men are created equal" extended the basic premise of equality—the right to vote—to merely one small and unrepresentative subset of its people.

THE SECOND AMENDMENT

Several years after the Constitution was enacted, the first ten amendments were ratified. These amendments are America's Bill of Rights.[11] Written primarily by James Madison, the

Bill of Rights limits what government can do to the people. The Bill of Rights was enacted in response to concerns that the new Constitution didn't sufficiently protect individual liberties. For example, the rights to speak and worship freely were cherished by Americans of all stripes yet left out of the Constitution. The 1st Amendment protects these rights. Likewise, the right to be free from government intrusions into the home was important to Americans still reeling from the English monarchy's disregard for civil liberties. The 4th Amendment thus prohibits unreasonable government searches and seizures.

The Bill of Rights includes essential prohibitions on government action that have long protected American citizens. But not everything about the Bill of Rights is positive. It also includes the 2nd Amendment, the right to keep and bear arms: "A well regulated Militia, being necessary to the security of a free State, the right of the people to keep and bear Arms, shall not be infringed."

The first thing to note about the 2nd Amendment is that— contrary to many assertions emanating from the left—it's just as legitimate and enforceable as any other duly enacted Constitutional provision. It's poorly drafted, ambiguous, and now (two-hundred-plus years later) stunningly outdated, to be sure. But so are numerous other Constitutional provisions, many of which 2nd Amendment critics righteously defend.

Liberal commentators argue, moreover, that conservative Supreme Court justices have construed the 2nd Amendment far beyond its fair definition. This may be true. Conservative majorities giddily expanded the 2nd Amendment to prohibit undue regulations on Americans' ability to possess guns at home (2008)[12] and in public (2022).[13] But overly broad Constitutional constructions by liberal justices are as American as apple pie. They've even invented rights not found in the Constitution at all (e.g., the right to privacy). It's highly unprincipled to criticize conservative justices for broadly construing Constitutional provisions one doesn't like, while, at the same time, cheering on liberal justices for broadly construing provisions one does. A coherent legal system requires judges to maintain a consistent interpretive philosophy—not ever-shifting modes of construction depending on the provision at issue.

So just because lots of people don't like the 2nd Amendment doesn't make it legally illegitimate or vanishingly narrow in scope. The real problem with the 2nd Amendment, rather, is its consequences. Broadly protecting gun rights leads to (surprise, surprise) a lot more guns. And a lot more guns lead to (surprise, surprise) a lot more gun violence. The 2nd Amendment is a rallying cry for America's gun-owning population—tens of millions strong—and breeds a dark culture of firearms and violence.

Indeed, perhaps the most disturbing widespread political belief in America today is that owning a gun is essential to maintaining individual liberty. Second Amendment enthusiasts think their liberty depends on their guns—the weapons they can use to protect themselves from the government. No, really. They do.

Then-Republican presidential candidate Vivek Ramaswamy articulated this view in an August 2023 speech to the National Rifle Association (NRA), the principal American gun-rights lobby. According to Ramaswamy,

"The Second Amendment is what made the Bill of Rights an American reality, not just an American dream."

This is, of course, utter hogwash. A huge population of gun-free Americans fully enjoy the Bill of Rights' protections. Ramaswamy's reasoning is as tortured as it is shameless: there's no logic or evidence suggesting a modern-day connection between gun ownership and political freedom. There is, however, iron-clad causation between the 2nd Amendment's broad protection of gun rights and gun violence. America's gun violence is worse than any other major democratic nation. The data are striking. Take a 2018 study of 195 countries and territories by the Institute for Health Metrics and Evaluation at the University of Washington.[14] It showed that in 2016, America's gun death rate far surpassed that of other developed democracies:

- America: 10.6 per 100,000 people
- Canada: 2.1
- Australia: 1.0
- France: 2.7
- Germany: 0.9
- Spain: 0.6

More than five Americans die from guns for every one Canadian killed by a gun. More than ten for every German. This travesty flows from the 2nd Amendment's legal and cultural power.

As Supreme Court justice Stephen Breyer wrote in his dissent from the court's 2022 opinion, striking down a New York gun law that dared to regulate gun possession outside the home: "The dangers posed by firearms can take many forms. Newspapers report mass shootings occurring at an entertainment district in Philadelphia, Pennsylvania (3 dead and 11 injured); an elementary school in Uvalde, Texas (21 dead); a supermarket in Buffalo, New York (10 dead and 3 injured); a series of spas in Atlanta, Georgia (8 dead); a busy street in an entertainment district of Dayton, Ohio (9 dead and 17 injured); a nightclub in Orlando, Florida (50 dead and 53 injured); a church in Charleston, South Carolina (9 dead); a movie theater in Aurora, Colorado (12 dead and 50 injured); an elementary school in Newtown, Connecticut (26 dead); and many, many more." He continued: "[M]ass shootings are just one part of the problem. Easy access to firearms can also make many other aspects of American life more dangerous. Consider, for example, the effect of guns on road rage."

Unsurprisingly, most Americans want stricter gun laws. According to Gallup in October 2023, the "latest update on Americans' opinions on gun laws finds a majority continuing to favor strengthening those laws. Fifty-six percent of U.S. adults say gun laws should be stricter, while 31% believe they should be kept as they are now and 12% favor less strict gun laws."

Unlike the Three-Fifths and Slave-Trade Clauses (addressed by the Civil-War amendments) and women's suffrage (addressed by the 19th Amendment), the 2nd Amendment's broad right to bear arms is still law. And it's not going away any time soon (no matter how many pithy law-review articles explain why it should). One of the Constitution's biggest flaws is how hard it is to amend. It requires two significant steps. Step one: "An amendment may be proposed by a two-thirds vote of both Houses of Congress, or, if two-thirds of the States request one, by a convention called for that purpose." And step two: "The amendment must then be ratified by three-fourths of the State legislatures, or three-fourths of conventions called in each State for ratification."[15] There have been only twenty-seven Constitutional amendments since 1787. As Supreme Court justice Antonin Scalia (typically a Constitutional cheerleader) admitted, amending the Constitution "ought to be hard, but not *that* hard."

When it comes to the 2nd Amendment, America's founders blew it. And it was a mistake that would stick. The right to "keep and bear arms" is an unfortunate, and enduring, blight in America's Constitutional constellation.

4

Constitutional Principles

"We have the oldest written Constitution still in force in the world,
and it starts out with three words: 'We, the people'"
Ruth Bader Ginsburg

What the United States Constitution got wrong is profound.
Yet so, too, is what the Constitution got right. Drawing on
the stark lessons of human history and the Enlightenment's
teachings, the founders' principal (and overlapping) aims
for the Constitution were threefold. The first was to create
a representative democracy that gave the American people
(narrowly defined) a stake in their own government. The
second aim was to prevent the concentration of government
power in too few hands. And the third was to accept and
harness the realities of human nature in a system that
would last.

DEMOCRACY
America is a representative, or republican, democracy. The
American people elect their representatives, who, in turn,

govern the American people. Members of the House of Representatives have two-year terms. Senators have six-year terms. The president has four-year terms and a two-term limit. Judges sit for life, subject to impeachment for bad acts. And members of the administrative state—America's vast federal bureaucracy—often hold their jobs for decades. A huge variety of similar substructures exist within each of the fifty states.

In a *direct* democracy, by contrast, the people decide directly—usually by majority vote—on government action, with no representative layer in between. Some states have mechanisms for direct democracy, including referendums the people vote on. But even referendums are usually narrow in substance and typically can be overruled by the legislature and voided by the courts. There is very little true direct democracy in America.

As James Madison explained in Federalist 55, a republican form of government strikes the right balance between empowering the people, on the one hand, and controlling the excesses of direct democracy, on the other. His assessment of human nature was sober and balanced: "As there is a degree of depravity in mankind which requires a certain degree of circumspection and distrust, so there are other qualities in human nature which justify a certain portion of esteem and confidence. Republican government presupposes the existence of these qualities in a higher degree than any other form."

This recognition by Madison and other founders that human nature is an intricate mix of positive and negative qualities pervades America's Constitutional design. Ironically, many of America's meanest critics—those who cast the harshest accusations against the country—root their condemnations in a view of human nature that's too kind. They mistakenly consider essential checks against the "depravity of mankind," like limiting unfettered democracy, to be unnecessary evils. This isn't to say that *all* people are depraved, of course. To the contrary, Madison's insight was, rather, that human history reveals that *enough* people are corrupt that a government must have broad safeguards to prevent *them* from obtaining too much power.

The founders were an ambitious lot. And they believed America would become a large nation. This made representative democracy a practical necessity. Madison again: "It is, that in a democracy, the people meet and exercise the government in person; in a republic, they assemble and administer it by their representatives and agents. A democracy, consequently, will be confined to a small spot. A republic may be extended over a large region."

America's representative democracy radically contrasts with not just history's monarchies but also the communist nations that arose after America's founding.

Communism has many definitions. The key distinction between communism generally and American democracy is this: in America, public power and private power are dispersed widely in the government and marketplace. While in communist nations, public power and private power (to the extent the latter exists at all) are concentrated in far fewer hands. The American version of democracy rejects all systems that concentrate power, however well-intentioned their architects' motivations may be.

The allure of concentrated power is that, in the right hands, it can rapidly and effectively promote human flourishing. As former president George W. Bush quipped: "If this were a dictatorship it would be a heck of a lot easier … as long as I'm the dictator. Hehehe." The problem, though, is that keeping concentrated power in the right hands only works in theory. While communism performs well on paper, history has shown—time and again—that it doesn't work. A steady stream of failed communist states litters recent history,[16] including Stalin's Russia, Mao's China, Pol Pot's Cambodia, Kim Jong Un's North Korea, and Fidel Castro's Cuba. These regimes each deployed the central combination of communism in practice: grand public statements appealing to inspirational ideals and murderous tyrants subjugating the people.

While few Americans support dictatorship or communism, socialism appeals to some. In September 2022, Pew Research found that "36% of U.S. adults say they view socialism somewhat (30%) or very (6%) positively." Socialism, of course, also has many definitions. And it's fertile ground for highly exaggerated rhetoric. "I myself don't use the word socialism," far-left United States Senator Bernie Sanders explained, "because people have been brainwashed into thinking socialism automatically means slave-labor camps, dictatorship and lack of freedom of speech." An accurate definition is less extreme. The core requirement of socialism is that wealth is broadly redistributed among the people. To the extent a socialist nation has a market-based economy and highly diverse government powers—and merely redistributes wealth significantly—it's consistent with America's design. (Contrary to strident assertions emanating from the right, a progressive tax code is not anti-American.) To the extent, however, that a socialist nation goes further and gives government control over the economy's means of production, or concentrates government power in limited hands, it conflicts with the American system.

Some Americans reject both democracy *and* socialism, and argue for alternative forms of government altogether. In his 2016 book *Against Democracy*, for example, Jason Brennan argues that democracy should be replaced with an "epistocracy." In an epistocracy, the votes of people who are knowledgeable about politics count more than those of people who aren't. According to Brennan, disenfranchising political ignorants would solve numerous societal problems. "[E]xcluding the bottom 80 percent of white voters from voting," for example, "might be just what poor blacks need." While the premise that American politics has a big ignorance problem is certainly true (see Chapter 7), this system has no chance in a country rooted in the tradition that every law-abiding adult has the right to vote.

In America, democracy has won. And in the broad context of human history, America's democracy has succeeded mightily. This is true not because it's without flaws. It has them. Nor is it true because hypothetical governments are always less attractive. Many have imagined far better forms of government than America's actual version. It's true, rather, because democracy is the most successful form of government, *in practice*, for maximizing human flourishing. Winston Churchill's famous observation was spot on:

"[D]emocracy is the worst form of Government, except for all those other forms that have been tried from time to time."

The first principle of American democracy—the premise upon which everything else rests—is that the people elect their representatives in free and fair elections. Given the importance of election integrity, politicians have long conceded elections even when they had a good-faith basis for questioning the outcome. Al Gore, for example, conceded to George W. Bush in 2000 after the Supreme Court ruled for Bush in litigation surrounding the election results in Florida. While Gore deeply believed he was the rightful winner, he nonetheless stepped aside. "Let there be no doubt, while I strongly disagree with the court's decision, I accept it," Gore said in his concession speech. "I accept the finality of this outcome which will be ratified next Monday in the Electoral College. And tonight, for the sake of our unity as a people and the strength of our democracy, I offer my concession."

That's how it had always worked. Losing candidates conceded close elections—for the country's sake—even if they thought that they had really won. Then came Donald Trump. As we'll explore in withering detail in Chapter 9, the 45th president of the United States tried to reverse the 2020 election from the Oval Office. After losing to Joe Biden, Trump lied repeatedly about the results. He asked state-government officials to "find" votes in his favor. He told Department of Justice leaders to lie and "just say the election was corrupt and leave the rest to me and the Republican Congressmen." He pushed state officials to manufacture fake slates of electors, which some did. He pressured then-Vice President Mike Pence to refuse to certify the election results.

And he organized a rally on January 6, 2021 that resulted in a mob of his supporters storming the United States Capitol as Congress attempted to certify the election results.

American politics overflows with false assertions and exaggerated rhetoric. Every. Single. Day. But it's stone-cold accurate to say this: Donald Trump tried to commit a coup after the 2020 presidential election.

The peaceful transfer of power after an election is the foundation of America's representative democracy. If the government is not reorganized to correspond with an election's results, then the people's will is void. Transferring power after elections is, indeed, central to America's emphatic rejection of kings and concentrated power. America's first president, George Washington, set the example early on by voluntarily resigning after two terms. "If he does that," King George III of England reportedly said when learning of Washington's plan to resign, "he will be the greatest man in the world."

George Washington voluntarily sacrificed his own power for the sake of his country. Donald Trump tried to sacrifice his country's democracy for the sake of his own power.

Trump failed. Miserably. The system withstood his assault. Joe Biden was inaugurated on time. And Trump is now facing multiple criminal trials addressing his malfeasance in office. But Trump's endless stream of lies about the 2020 presidential election still courses through the body politic. And he's still the Republican party's undisputed champion as the 2024 presidential election approaches. The predicament is startling: the central platform of one of America's two pre-eminent political parties is fundamentally at odds with the first principle of how America works—that government is reorganized after elections to reflect the people's will.

SEPARATION OF POWERS

Election integrity has indeed been critical to America's success. So has the separation of powers. The founders knew that if America's representative democracy was to last it had to distribute power broadly. They had one obsession above all others: to prevent concentrated government power. And rightly so. History revealed the danger of kings and tyrants ruling from a single throne.

There is, indeed, a natural tendency in all government systems for power to consolidate. In his presidential farewell address, George Washington warned the brand-new republic of this age-old threat: "The spirit of encroachment tends to consolidate the powers of all the departments in one, and thus to create, whatever the form of government, a real despotism. A just estimate of that love of power, and proneness to abuse it, which predominates in the human heart, is sufficient to satisfy us of the truth of this position."

Washington was sober about human nature: people love power. The more they have it, the more they want it—and the more of it they are able to obtain. Again, this propensity might not be true for everyone. But it's true for enough people that a well-constituted government must guard against it—firmly.

Washington continued: "The necessity of reciprocal checks in the exercise of political power, by dividing and distributing it into different depositaries, and constituting each the guardian of the public weal against invasions by the others, has been evinced by experiments ancient and modern … To preserve them must be as necessary as to institute them."

Separating power among the branches is more than just one discrete element of American government. It's a central premise upon which Americans' fundamental rights and privileges depend. As Antonin Scalia put it: "It is the structure of government, its Constitution in the real sense of that word, that ultimately preserves or destroys freedom. A bill of rights is no more than ink on paper unless it is addressed to a government so constituted that no part of it can obtain excessive power."

As noted, the first way the founders divided and distributed power was by erecting three independent and coequal branches of the federal government:

- Article I of the Constitution gives Congress the legislative power: "All legislative Powers herein granted shall be vested in a Congress of the United States, which shall consist of a Senate and House of Representatives."
- Article II gives the president the executive power: "The executive Power shall be vested in a President of the United States of America."
- Article III gives the courts the judicial power: "The judicial Power of the United States, shall be vested in one Supreme Court, and in such inferior Courts as the Congress may from time to time ordain and establish."

This architecture works. The branches are an intricate, interconnected web of powers that balance and check each other from myriad angles and directions. While power ebbs and flows amongst the branches based on time, circumstance, and subject matter, no single branch has taken an overriding position in American government.

Even the most influential single actor, the president, has sharp limits on his powers, especially domestically. The founders' deep-seated fear of kings permeates the everyday workings of the executive branch. The president needs majorities in both houses of Congress to pass legislation. The courts can strike down the president's initiatives if they transgress the Constitution or duly enacted legislation. The president is subject to Congress's investigatory powers—in both chambers—including impeachment and removal. Even the administrative state of executive agencies often acts independently from—and fiercely at odds with—the president. The Department of Justice, for example, can investigate and potentially prosecute a sitting president. And executive branch actors can be hauled into court by a state, a municipality, or even a single American citizen.

Congress, for its part, can't pass legislation without a presidential signature—unless they override a presidential veto with a two-thirds majority (which is very rare). Congressional legislation must be implemented and enforced by the executive branch and can be, and frequently is, voided by the courts. And while the Constitution gives Congress the power to declare war, in practice it's the president—the commander-in-chief—who decides how and when to commit US troops.

The judiciary is likewise checked and balanced by the other branches. Federal judges must be nominated by the president and confirmed by the Senate. Judges sit for life, on good behavior, and are subject to Congressional impeachment. Congress can create, and eliminate, the lower courts (those other than the Supreme Court) and it sets the jurisdiction, or powers, of all courts through legislation. And judges are limited under the Constitution to deciding the "cases and controversies" that come before them; they formulate policy neither broadly nor on a blank slate.

The net impact of this design is that each branch is very powerful and influential, but none more so than the other to any material degree. The one exception is the executive branch in foreign affairs. The exigencies and complexities of foreign policy have led to more executive power than was envisioned in the Constitution.

Today, critics bemoan how these checks and balances cause the federal government to move slowly. They have a point. American government is often gridlocked—allowing significant policy failures to persist. And some of this can be attributed to the separation of powers. (As we will see in Part Two, Chapters 7 and 8, political dysfunction plays the primary role.) It would be easier at times if, for example, the president could take bold domestic action without legislative authority. Two recent battles illustrate the point. President Biden's initiative to cancel hundreds of billions of dollars in student-loan debt would have helped millions of borrowers in need. In Chapter 8 we'll see how this debt places a crushing burden on younger generations. But Congress's legislative grant was too narrow to support Biden's ambitious program. The legislative power granted to Congress under Article I would be nullified if presidents could simply legislate from the

White House. And the Supreme Court struck the program down in October 2022, reaffirming the separation of powers and requiring *both* Congress and the president to authorize federal law and policy through duly enacted legislation.[17]

Earlier that year the Supreme Court also struck down Biden's attempt to address another major public-policy concern. This time climate change. The court ruled that the Environmental Protection Agency went beyond its statutory authority with its decision to require private enterprises to utilize clean energy.[18] Chief Justice John Roberts, writing for the court, stated, "A decision of such magnitude and consequence rests [not with the executive branch but rather] with Congress itself, or an agency acting pursuant to a clear delegation from that representative body."

Politicians and pundits also blast the balance of power between the branches when they don't like who has the upper hand. After Donald Trump appointed three conservative Supreme Court justices—sending the court careening to the right—liberals howled that Biden and Congressional Democrats should stack the court in their favor. The aim was to regain a liberal majority. Taking the long view, liberal justice Stephen Breyer warned against this encroachment: "Well, if one party could do it, I guess another party could do it ... On the surface it seems to me you start changing all these things around, and people will lose trust in the court." Breyer, appointed by Democrat Bill Clinton, continued: "I'm there for everybody. I'm not just there for the Democrats. I'm not just there for the Republicans. And I'm not just there because a president was a Democrat who appointed me."

Likewise, excited critics of executive overreach inevitably emerge—as night follows day—from the opposing side of the political divide. George W. Bush's aggressive approach to fighting terrorism, including waterboarding enemy detainees, was excoriated as a dangerous expansion of presidential power, evading Congressional oversight and violating judicial precedent. Author Scott Horton expressed common sentiments: "We may not have realized it, but in the period from late 2001–January 19, 2009 [Bush's presidency], this country was a dictatorship. That was thanks to secret memos crafted deep inside the Justice Department that effectively trashed the Constitution."

Bush's successor, Barack Obama, promised to change all this. As a presidential candidate, Obama said that "the biggest problems we're facing right now are to do with George Bush trying to bring more and more power into the executive branch and not go through Congress at all. And that's what I intend to reverse when I am President of the United States of America."

As the founders would have predicted, however, the desire to exert power in office overrode candidate Obama's aspirations. Stanford law professor and former federal appellate judge Michael McConnell outlined President Obama's expansive use of executive power:

Barack Obama was no less assertive in using his executive powers—maybe more so than President Bush, and not just in the national security arena, but in many arenas. He talked about using what he called 'the pen and the phone' to make national policy outside of Congress. Some of the notable instances in that administration were an undeclared air war in Libya, orders granting lawful status to more than 4 million undocumented workers after Congress had voted that proposal down, environmental regulations stretching the terms of the statutes, some $7 billion in subsidies for insurance companies that had not been voted for by Congress, and, dear to the hearts of many college students, a 'Dear Colleague' letter announcing the regulation of the sex lives of college students.

The reaction of most Bush critics to Obama's aggressive executive assertions? Hardly a peep.

The biggest contemporary flashpoint surrounding the separation of powers is impeachment. For several decades now, the opposition party in Congress has consistently used impeachment—or its threat—to undermine the duly elected president. Republicans went after Democrat Bill Clinton with vengeance in the 90s for his indiscretions with a White House intern and his associated perjury.[19] Clinton's offenses weren't trivial: having sexual relations with an intern (in the Oval Office no less) was reckless and beneath the presidency. And lying under oath, as Clinton did, was criminal. But the Republicans' impeachment spectacle—a multi-year, $52 million[20] bonanza—was a ruthlessly disproportionate response. And the true victim wasn't Clinton. It was the American people, whose government was consumed for years with salacious drama, prurient interest, and tribal warfare, all at the expense of better governance.

Two decades later it was the Democrats' turn to overreach.[21] They salivated over impeaching Donald Trump from well before he took office. As Emily Jane Fox wrote in *Vanity Fair* on December 15, 2016, a month before Trump assumed the presidency, "Democrats are paving the way to impeach Donald Trump." Again, Trump's offenses weren't trivial: pressuring Ukrainian President Volodymyr Zelenskyy to investigate Trump's political rival Joe Biden—and withholding Congressionally authorized Ukrainian aid in the process—was abhorrent. But Democrats undermined the process from the outset by transparently obsessing over getting Trump, rather than uncovering the truth about what happened. Many central questions about the underlying events remain unanswered, buried under the rubble of partisan assertion and innuendo. And a fiercely anti-Trump zealot, Adam Schiff, even ran the Democrat's impeachment effort—feverishly amplifying facts that hurt Trump while trying to erase those that helped him.

Impeachment is, indeed, a solemn Constitutional proceeding that must be handled with temperance and discretion. Only "high crimes and misdemeanors" under the Constitution's Impeachment Clause give rise to impeachment.[22] If Congress removes a president from office without a valid Constitutional basis, the separation of powers is eviscerated. Indeed, the only time all Americans come together and vote on the same question is the presidential election. The entirety of the Constitution's Article II power, moreover, is reposed in the president: "The executive Power shall be vested in a President of the United States of America." An improper impeachment would thus negate the people's will more so than virtually any other act of government. And while requiring two-thirds of the Senate to convict and remove a president is an effective check on abuse,[23] unscrupulous impeachments in the House undermine the presidency's legitimacy and effectiveness.

Overreaching impeachments, moreover, have set in motion a pernicious cycle. As I wrote about Trump's first impeachment in October 2019, "The Democrats must remember that they are writing a rule book that will eventually apply to them, too. Every step the Democrats take to remove Mr. Trump from office can—and perhaps likely will—be used against them in the future. If a Democrat is elected president in 2020, Congressional Republicans will be salivating at the prospect of impeachment. The more the Democrats push the limits now, the less ability they would have, then, to resist impeachment." Sure enough, in December 2023, Republicans formally began an impeachment inquiry into Joe Biden's business dealings with his son Hunter. There's no evidence suggesting Joe committed a "high crime or misdemeanor" under the Constitution.

My admonition was hardly a great insight. Everyone paying attention knew what was coming. That's how US politics works in the twenty-first century: every infraction from one tribe must be met with an even greater offense by the other.

If Congress was truly respecting the separation of powers, then impeachment would be considered a last resort, not a first impulse. The goal of the proceedings would be to uncover the relevant facts, not manufacture a winning case. And the duly elected president's legitimacy would be weighed heavily, not cast aside.

Richard Nixon's impeachment proceedings in 1974 illustrate how the system is supposed to work. Nixon was accused of ordering subordinates to break into the

Democratic National Committee's headquarters at the Watergate Hotel in Washington and steal confidential information. The alleged crime was significant. The evidence pointing to Nixon's guilt was material. And here's the key: Congress undertook a respectful, bipartisan effort to uncover the truth. They weren't trying to destroy Nixon. Nor were they trying to reverse the results of an election. They were, instead, trying to figure out what had happened and address Nixon's misconduct with the country's best interests in mind. With the evidence mounting against him—and numerous Congressional Republicans indicating they would vote to oust him—Nixon resigned from office.

Then there was Donald Trump's second impeachment by the House of Representatives. This time, Trump's offenses weren't just non-trivial. They were immense. His malfeasance in office after the 2020 presidential election was a "high crime or misdemeanor" under any definition. And most of the evidence against him was already in the public domain. The only threat to the integrity of the impeachment process was *not* seeking his removal from office. While the proceedings were hurried and mostly partisan, in part due to the limited time before Trump's term ended, the contrast with Trump's first impeachment was enormous.

The three branches of America's federal government are supposed to check and balance each other, with energy but also with discretion. The separation of powers requires Congress to pursue impeachment only when the president actually commits an impeachable offense. America doesn't tolerate kings. But nor does it gain from a president under siege.

FEDERALISM

The Constitution doesn't just separate the federal government's powers into three coequal branches. It also divides up authority between the federal government and the states. The 10th Amendment reserves all powers not expressly outlined in the Constitution to the states and to the people: "The powers not delegated to the United States by the Constitution, nor prohibited by it to the States, are reserved to the States respectively, or to the people."

While the precise balance consistently shifts, many fundamental laws and policies shaping Americans' daily lives are local. State and municipal governments have primary responsibility for their constituents' safety, education, and general welfare. This is by design. As James Madison explained: "The powers delegated by the proposed Constitution to the federal government are few and defined. Those which are to remain in the State governments are numerous and indefinite."

Federalism is based on three simple ideas. The first is that having strong state governments counterbalances the federal government, which always threatens to become too powerful. Alexander Hamilton explained that rivalry, in this instance, is desirable. "This balance between the National and State governments ought to be dwelt on with peculiar attention, as it is of the utmost importance. It forms a double security to the people. If one encroaches on their rights they will find a powerful protection in the other. Indeed, they will both be prevented from overpassing their Constitutional limits by a certain rivalship, which will ever subsist between them."

The tension between federal and state government can be fierce. Under the Constitution's Supremacy Clause, duly enacted federal laws trump state laws. But to be duly enacted, a federal law must have a valid and express Constitutional basis. Presidents and Congress often overreach and improperly impose broad federal policies on states and localities.

Recent battles over immigration highlight the dynamics. In 2017, for example, Donald Trump issued an executive order to withhold federal funding from sanctuary cities—those cities that shield undocumented immigrants within their borders from federal law and deportation. As we'll see in Chapter 8, this order was one of Trump's many harsh, anti-immigrant initiatives. Numerous sanctuary cities, including San Francisco, sued Trump, arguing that taking away their duly authorized federal funding was unconstitutional. As San Francisco City Attorney Dennis Herrera explained, the federal government "can't put a gun to the head of states and localities to get them to comply with what you might want at the federal level." At the time, San Francisco was shielding about 30,000 undocumented residents and was receiving about $1.2 billion annually in federal funding. Herrera said Trump's order was unconstitutional because it "tries to turn city and state employees into federal immigration enforcers." After years of litigation, San Francisco ultimately won the case when, in 2021, the Biden administration didn't appeal an appellate court's ruling in the city's favor.[24]

The second idea underpinning federalism is that state-government officials are better at managing their localities than far-away federal officials in Washington DC, most of whom focus disproportionately on their own home districts.

Many arguments in political science are complicated. This one is easy: it's better for your neighbor to govern your neighborhood than a distant stranger. Look no further than education, where the federal government has imposed standardized rules for student education. Local school boards, teachers, and parents have long felt that these standards— one-size-fits-all nationally—are misplaced, misguided, and counterproductive, taking local context and sensibility out of students' curriculum.[25]

Finally, keeping important government work local allows the people to look after the government—not just the other way around. Thomas Jefferson recognized this virtue: "[T]he States can best govern our home concerns and the general government our foreign ones. I wish, therefore ... never to see all offices transferred to Washington, where, further withdrawn from the eyes of the people, they may more secretly be bought and sold at market." This consideration, too, is rooted in common sense. It's far easier to understand what your local representatives are up to than federal officials, most of whom have never even visited your hometown.

These three simple considerations make federalism a key, if often overlooked, part of how America works. Yet the politics surrounding federalism are often complicated and divisive. And they reveal a backwards impulse pulsating through the body politic: short-sighted partisans are far more concerned with policy *outcomes* than government *process*, including which level of government (state or federal) should be at work. The problem with this pathology is that over time getting the process right—and sticking with it—is essential. People need a shared set of rules that binds them together to function well in a civilized society. Having everyone lurching around trying to change the rules—depending on the desired end result—is deeply counterproductive.

With federalism, drawing the right lines can be hard, as two contrasting considerations are often at odds. Giving states too much autonomy leaves local minorities vulnerable to abuse. If the federal government doesn't step in to protect them, no one will. Yet giving the federal government too much authority diminishes the vital role local officials should play in formulating policy. Far-away officials ignorant of the facts on the ground shouldn't dictate the affairs of local communities.

The abuse in the American South during Jim Crow was an example of states having too much autonomy in the federalist system. After the Supreme Court's ruling in *Brown v. Board of Education* (1954)[26] required racial integration in schools, for example, southern states stridently resisted. Many schools simply refused to admit Black children. The federal government had no choice but to intervene and stop the abuse. Ultimately, President Eisenhower deployed armed federal troops in Alabama to force compliance with the court's decision.

Today's political battles involving federalism are also fierce. Take the Voting Rights Act, which protects southern minorities from state-sanctioned electoral abuses.[27] The Act addressed an important problem when it was enacted in 1965: southern states had a long history of limiting the franchise for Black Americans. At the same time, however, the federal intrusion into state government is profound: federal officials in Washington DC, often from a rival political party, telling local governments how to run their own elections is hard to square with the 10th Amendment. In a variety of recent decisions, the Supreme Court has narrowed the Act's scope, providing more autonomy to state election officials as racist voting discrimination has decreased.

Federalism concerns also underpin today's political warfare over abortion. On one side: tens of millions of Americans believe that abortion is a fundamental Constitutional right and states mustn't limit a woman's rights to choose whether, and when, to have an abortion. On the other: tens of millions believe states must regulate abortion and protect unborn fetuses.

Who should decide this immensely charged issue? Should all fifty states be free to go their own way? Or should the federal government impose a uniform standard?

In 1973 in *Roe v. Wade*, the Supreme Court took jurisdiction over this question. (There is more on this case, and the court, in the next chapter.) The court held that the federal Constitution did in fact contain the right to an abortion and therefore that states couldn't abolish or unduly limit the procedure. Several subsequent cases tinkered with the standard, ultimately preventing states from outlawing abortions before the third trimester. Then in 2022, with a brand-new conservative majority, the court overruled *Roe* and sent the issue back to the states, eliminating the fifty-year-old Constitutional right to an abortion.

Conservatives celebrated this expansion of federalism. Liberals seethed. And a predictable inconsistency arose: many conservatives who opposed *Roe* on federalism grounds called for a national ban on abortion now that, according to them, the Constitution no longer forbade such legislation. Principled conservatives (a rare species these days) shook their heads: it's hard to imagine anything more inconsistent with the 10th Amendment's reservation of powers to the states than a national ban dictating women's reproductive choices.

Like voting rights, abortion is a very difficult problem. How can every American be treated fairly when a woman's body is at odds with a fetus's life? Likewise, how can southern minorities be protected and—at the same time—local governments empowered? As we'll explore further in Chapter 7, anyone who thinks there are easy answers to these hard questions isn't grasping their complexity. The partisans look foolish in their zeal.

The controversies surrounding where to draw the line between state and federal power will never stop. And those on the losing side of disputes will always bemoan the system. But federalism is nonetheless an essential pillar of how America works—a true safeguard against the centralized government power that plagued human history and that the founders were so focused on preventing.

FREE SPEECH

History reveals that free speech is also vital to human freedom. Tyrants don't just concentrate power; they eliminate dissent and monopolize ideas. Violence within and between nations increases when governments stifle communication. And restricting the marketplace of ideas decreases innovations that promote human flourishing.

Another essential principle defining how America works is thus the strong protection of free speech. The 1st Amendment to the Constitution prevents Congress from abridging speech: "Congress Shall Make No Law ... Abridging the Freedom of Speech, or of the Press ..."[28] The Supreme Court has ruled that this prohibition applies to all levels of government: federal, state, and local. And while private actors (such as individuals and companies) may limit speech, a strong national ethos has long favored a free and robust marketplace of ideas. As George Orwell explained in 1945, it's the people's ethos that matters most: "If large numbers of people believe in freedom of speech, there will be freedom of speech, even if the law forbids it. But if public opinion is sluggish, inconvenient minorities will be persecuted, even if laws exist to protect them."

Perhaps free speech's biggest virtue is checking and restraining government power. Fear of public criticism deters malfeasance in office. And a robust press uncovers, and therefore reduces, government abuse. Allowing outsiders to investigate and criticize the government is critical. America's press (the "Fourth Branch" of government) consistently confirms this truth. In the 1970s, for example, *Washington Post* reporters uncovered President Richard Nixon's direct involvement in the criminal Watergate scheme. After the *Post*'s extensive coverage of the scandal, the bipartisan consensus arose in Congress that Nixon had committed an impeachable offense. Shortly thereafter, he became the first US president to resign from office.

Free speech also reduces civil strife by allowing people to express their views without resorting to physical violence. This cathartic venting is crucial. When speech is stifled, grievance bottles up, expands, and intensifies. Violence becomes more likely.

The free marketplace of ideas, moreover, is essential to discovering the truth. John Stuart Mill put it best: "The peculiar evil of silencing the expression of an opinion is that it is robbing the human race; posterity as well as the existing generation; those who dissent from the opinion, still more than those who hold it. If the opinion is right, they are deprived of the opportunity of exchanging error for truth: if wrong, they lose, what is almost as great a benefit, the clearer perception and livelier impression of truth, produced by its collision with error." US Supreme Court justice Oliver Wendell Holmes Jr. agreed. In *Abrams v. United States* (1919), Holmes dissented from the court's ruling upholding the conviction of an anti-war anarchist. According to Holmes, the anarchist should have been allowed to speak his mind. "[W]hen men have realized that time has upset many fighting faiths, they may come to believe even more than they believe the very foundations of their own conduct that the ultimate good desired is better reached by free trade in ideas—that the best test of truth is the power of the thought to get itself accepted in the competition of the market."

The right to speak freely has been key to America's success. It is not absolute, however. In *Brandenburg v. Ohio* (1969), the Supreme Court held that the 1st Amendment doesn't protect speech "directed to inciting or producing imminent lawless action and is likely to incite or produce such action." This makes good sense. The 1st Amendment isn't a license to break the law or harm one's fellow citizens.

But the standard isn't always easy to apply. Take, for example, then-President Donald Trump's speech on January 6, 2021. As we'll explore further in Chapter 9, Trump held a rally several blocks from the United States Capitol while Congress was officially certifying Joe Biden's 2020 presidential election victory. Trump whipped the crowd into a frenzy with one incendiary assertion after another:

- "We won this election, and we won it by a landslide."
- "We will stop the steal."
- "We will never give up. We will never concede. It doesn't happen."
- "You don't concede when there's theft involved. Our country has had enough. We will not take it anymore."
- "You will have an illegitimate president. That is what you will have, and we can't let that happen."
- "If you don't fight like hell, you're not going to have a country any more."
- "We're going to walk down to the Capitol and we're going to cheer on our brave senators and Congressmen and women, and we're probably not going to be cheering so much for some of them."

Trump's speech was typically confused and disjointed. He also encouraged the crowd to protest peacefully: "I know that everyone here will soon be marching over to the Capitol building to peacefully and patriotically make your voices heard."

Immediately after the speech, Trump's supporters stormed the Capitol in a violent attempt to shut down Congress's certification of Joe Biden's victory. Blood spilled on the center of American government as the mob broke into the building, halted the proceedings, and sent shocked legislators scrambling for safety in underground bunkers.

Republican Congresswoman Liz Cheney described Trump's role on January 6 as follows:

> January 6th and the lies that led to insurrection have put two and a half centuries of Constitutional democracy at risk ... President Trump believed his supporters at the Capitol, and I quote, 'were doing what they should be doing'. This is what he told his staff as they pleaded with him to call off the mob ... On this point, there is no room for debate. Those who invaded our Capitol and battled law enforcement for hours were motivated by what President Trump had told them: that the election was stolen, and that he was the rightful president. President Trump summoned the mob, assembled the mob and lit the flame of this attack.

It's hard to argue with Cheney's characterization. But was Trump's speech nonetheless protected by the 1st Amendment? Or did he incite imminent illegal violence and therefore break the law?

Despite the horrific consequences of his supporters' violence—and the criminality of his post-election behavior in other respects—Trump's speech was protected. He didn't explicitly call for violence and he did caution his fans to protest peacefully. And while his lies were sinister, he didn't call for imminent lawless action. His speech was, indeed, quintessentially political speech—an incumbent president speaking to supporters in the public square about highly charged political issues. The key consideration is this: if Trump's speech was not protected by the 1st Amendment—and therefore deemed illegal—it would substantially chill politicians' public statements going forward. This core political speech is central to the free marketplace of ideas. Politicians must be encouraged to speak openly and passionately to their constituents, not deterred from doing so. Policing and criminalizing politicians' speech—even speech riddled with lies—would do a lot more harm than good.

Department of Justice Special Counsel Jack Smith agrees. Smith declined to charge Trump for his January 6 speech in a July 2023 indictment that does charge Trump for numerous crimes relating to the 2020 presidential election.[29] (There is more on this in Chapter 9.) Trump's speech was deceitful, destructive, and dangerous—but it was protected speech under the 1st Amendment.

As it should be. Having very broad protections for political speech is essential. A simple litmus test applies: if speech that deeply offends, disturbs, even scares many people isn't fundamentally protected—with room to spare—then the freedom of speech is abridged.

America is backsliding with its approach to speech. Today, more and more people are trying to silence voices they disagree with. The trend started on university campuses decades ago. As long-time professor Thomas Sowell put it, "There are no institutions in America where free speech is more severely restricted than in our politically correct colleges and universities."

In my own experience at the University of California, Los Angeles, in the early 2000s, I saw first-hand a deep antipathy to expressing disfavored views. Almost all my professors were very far to the left. Paul Von Blum, for example, was a wonderfully likable and charismatic professor—a brilliant mind and powerful orator. Medium in stature and build, with wavy gray hair and fiercely intense blue eyes, Von Blum was very popular with students. He was also a fierce leftist ideologue. His lectures were thundering anti-American rants punctuated by spit-flying howls and boosted by the occasional softball question from an adoring student lobbed up to him on stage from an overflowing lecture hall. His class was, more than anything, a cathartic platform for him to vent his politics.

The stunning thing about his pedagogy was this: if a question pushed against or tested his theories he got agitated. He didn't welcome debate; he hated it. Viscerally. He would even twist unfriendly questions (which became rarer and rarer as the semester wore on) into friendlier versions and then ask his students if that's what they really meant to ask.

During one typical diatribe he was blasting America's military for its hierarchical structure. Something like: "Soldiers have no due-process rights and no ability to question or challenge the chain of command; it's little different from a prison." I asked him: "Don't you think having a hierarchy is important in order to keep the troops functioning efficiently and in line with their orders from the democratically elected commander-in-chief?" This rude interruption to his train of thought was not well received. He replied: "Absolutely *not*. Setting aside the validity of the premise of your question—that we need a military at all—there are ways to function efficiently *and also* provide rights to soldiers, most of whom come from underprivileged backgrounds." Without offering me a chance to respond, he turned and walked away across the stage in the opposite direction, resuming his monologue.

Then there was adjunct professor Jeffrey Valle. Like Von Blum, Valle was nice, charismatic, and brilliant. Thin, with short brown hair and a gentle, sophisticated demeanor, Valle was an attorney at the leading international law firm Skadden Arps. The name of his class was something like *Communications 101: Propaganda in the Media*. The main book was *Manufacturing Consent* by Edward Herman and Noam Chomsky. There were other readings, too. And every single reading and all lectures came from exactly one narrow perspective: left-wing, anti-establishment, anti-business. The material all converged on the exact same thesis: the media is controlled by, and biased in favor of, right-wing corporate interests.

Valle was less hostile to questions than Von Blum. But in his gentle, charming way, when dissenting comments and skeptical questions arose he used them to further his point. Instead of giving a fair shake to his much-younger students, he subtly twisted their questions into fodder for his own opinions. I told Valle after the semester that it was hypocritical to have a class focused exclusively on the thesis that it's dangerous to have the media present things from only one narrow point of view—while the class presented everything *from only one narrow point of view*. Many people have different perspectives on the media, I continued, including long-time journalist Bernard Goldberg, author of the *New York Times* bestselling book *Bias*. Goldberg's book argued that the media had a strong left-wing ideological bias. Setting aside whether Goldberg's views were correct or not, he was an expert in the relevant subject matter expressing an opinion shared by many. To Valle's credit, *Bias* was on his reading list the following semester, though I doubt it was presented objectively in his lectures.

That kind of minor concession was rare. Most professors were proud and strident in their orthodoxy. The UCLA campus was anything other than a free marketplace of ideas. At the time, I found this climate very surprising. Wasn't a university supposed to be a place where free speech was respected? Wouldn't a free marketplace of ideas help students learn? That was the whole point, I thought. The hostility to opposing views was truly perplexing. It was also odd to me that brilliant people like Von Blum and Valle were so clearly biased in some instances. (As I learned later and examine in Chapter 6, bias among highly intelligent people is common.) But I also assumed that this dysfunctional brand of ideological extremism was limited to the campus and not something that had (or was likely to) spread into broader society.

I was right for about a decade. But by 2015 the insanity of the campus was invading broader society. Hostility to divergent views has now infected many American institutions, from corporations and non-profits to the media and government agencies. The tactics are extreme: attacking speakers on social media; running people from their jobs; denying tenure to professors; shouting down speakers with the wrong views; threatening administrators with the wrong rules; boycotting companies affiliated with the wrong people.[30] More and more Americans, disproportionately on the left, are casting aside age-old principles valuing free speech in favor of short-sighted, knee-jerk prohibitions on speakers they don't like. As Andrew Sullivan put it: "We're all on campus now."

Examples of this "cancel culture" involving three of America's most influential institutions underscore the problem. Shortly after I left UCLA in 2005, Larry Summers was forced to resign as Harvard's president. During his rocky tenure, Summers alienated numerous factions within the Harvard faculty. The last straw was a speech Summers gave in which he suggested that women's underrepresentation in science may be due, in part, to "issues of intrinsic aptitude." Summers posited that the very upper end of science aptitude (comprising the extreme outliers) was disproportionately male. About his theory, Summers noted: "I would like nothing better than to be proved wrong, because I would like nothing better than for these problems to be addressable simply by everybody understanding what they are, and working very hard to address them."

Setting aside whether Summers' argument was correct or not, his thesis was rooted in hard data and sober analysis. It wasn't discriminatory; no matter how you define various groups of people (by race, class, gender, or otherwise), you will always find minor differences at the margins. Groups of people are different. Men are better, on average, than women at some things. And vice versa. That's the truth. And that's okay. It all washes out in the aggregate. Pretending otherwise stifles the marketplace of ideas, distorts perceptions of reality, and increases (rather than decreases) societal tension. As long as everyone is treated and valued equally—which is essential—serious questions about human differences should be invited and respected, not silenced.

Exemplifying how "cancel culture" moved beyond the campus, in 2017 Google fired software engineer James Damore for echoing Summers' views. In a memorandum posted to Google's internal employee network titled *Google's Ideological Echo Chamber*,[31] Damore explained his view that there are numerous inherent differences between men and women.

According to Damore:

> I value diversity and inclusion, am not denying that sexism exists, and don't endorse using stereotypes. When addressing the gap in representation in the population, we need to look at population level differences in distributions. If we can't have an honest discussion about this, then we can never truly solve the problem. Psychological safety is built on mutual respect and acceptance, but unfortunately our culture of shaming and misrepresentation is disrespectful and unaccepting of anyone outside its echo chamber. Despite what the public response seems to have been, I've gotten many personal messages from fellow Googlers expressing their gratitude for bringing up these very important issues which they agree with but would never have the courage to say or defend because of our shaming culture and the possibility of being fired. This needs to change.

Like Summers, Damore's premises may (or may not) have been correct. But punishing him for respectfully expressing himself about an important subject was wrong.

Then, a few years later, the "Fourth Branch" of government took its turn. The *New York Times* opinion editor and writer Adam Rubenstein resigned in December 2020, six months after he edited a piece by Arkansas' Republican Senator Tom Cotton. (The *Times* fired Rubenstein's boss, James Bennet, shortly after the piece ran.) Cotton's column argued for President Trump to "send in the troops" to quell violent left-wing political protests in numerous cities. According to Cotton, "One thing above all else will restore order to our streets: an overwhelming show of force to disperse, detain and ultimately deter lawbreakers. But local law enforcement in some cities desperately needs backup, while delusional politicians in other cities refuse to do what's necessary to uphold the rule of law."

As former *Times* editor Bari Weiss wrote about Rubenstein's resignation, "Adam was hung out to dry by his own colleagues. Then he and his work were lied about, including in [a] mendacious editor's note."

Cotton may (or may not) have been wrong to call for troops. But the country's leading newspaper shouldn't punish an editor for publishing speech from a sitting senator about an important issue of public concern—even, indeed especially, a controversial one.

Many others have been punished for legitimate political speech, too. (San Francisco's school board even cancelled—it's true—George Washington, Abraham Lincoln, and Thomas Jefferson by wiping their names from schools because of "ties to racism" and "dishonorable legacies.")[32] But these three examples highlight the fundamental danger of silencing speech. Harvard is the crown jewel of America's higher education. It shapes the minds of America's brightest students, and its professors are influential thought leaders. Google dominates the flow of online information. By adjusting its algorithms it can—and does—fundamentally alter what billions of people see and know about the world.[33] And the *New York Times*, more than any other institution, sets the agenda for the national political debate.

These three titans fundamentally shape the contours of America's public square. For them to punish speech that, while controversial, is essential to a free marketplace of ideas and the pursuit of truth isn't just mistaken. It's dangerous. Harvard, Google, and the *New York Times* have outsized influence in American society. But their leaders do not have a monopoly on wisdom.

The way to counteract speech you don't like is to explain why it's wrong. Silencing speech and canceling speakers is deeply counterproductive for three reasons. First, the censors don't have more wisdom than the censored. They often have less. Censorship can just as easily muzzle important truths as it can silence subversive lies. History is filled with minority views that eventually became gospel (every person should be equal under the law) and popular ideas that eventually became abominations (certain races are inferior to others).

Second, accuracy matters. Silencing speech is often motivated by the desire to preserve cherished narratives that are empirically incorrect. Bad ideas love nothing more than a marketplace hostile to new ones. This is especially dangerous in a representative democracy like America, where the views of constituents inform and even dictate the official acts of their elected representatives. Speaking accurately should be encouraged, even if it upsets people. This doesn't mean speakers should over-emphasize hard truths and controversial ideas. Or exaggerate them. Or fail to place them in context. Or fail to show decency when expressing them. Or assert them at the wrong time, in the wrong place, or in the wrong manner. But if you navigate all that and merely state objective facts, pose empirically valid questions, or offer reasoned conclusions, then you should come under no scorn. There needs to be space in the public square for people to speak accurately.

Even if it hurts.

Finally, silencing speech is a slippery slope. What starts at the university can eventually go mainstream. And what goes mainstream can eventually infect the highest echelons of government. Once this happens, a straight line to tyranny emerges. If the President of the United States were ever to punish disfavored speakers like the Harvard faculty, Google's CEO, or the *New York Times'* publisher, the nation would be in peril. Echoing the founders' fear of kings, then-US President Harry Truman put it plainly in 1950: "Once a government is committed to the principle of silencing the voice of opposition, it has only one way to go, and that is down the path of increasingly repressive measures, until it becomes a source of terror to all its citizens and creates a country where everyone lives in fear."

This of course hasn't happened. And America still has more protections for speech than most countries. But given the vital importance of robust speech to the functioning of democratic society, America's twenty-first-century free-speech free fall is deeply concerning.

It must not be allowed to get worse.

5

Essential Traditions

"Independence means voluntary restraints and discipline,
voluntary acceptance of the rule of law"
Mahatma Gandhi

These principles enshrined in the United States Constitution—
representative democracy, separation of powers, federalism,
and free speech—have helped define the American experience.
But there are also essential traditions shaping how America
works (for better and for worse) not found in the Constitution.
While they do not carry the force of Constitutional law, they
are just as central to the American experiment.

THE TWO-PARTY SYSTEM
The worst such tradition is the two-party political system.
In America there are two juggernaut political parties: the
Democrats and the Republicans. Third parties sprout up
occasionally, but they never dent this duopoly. As will be
analyzed in Part Two, the two-party system dramatically
worsens the tribalism plaguing American politics.

Just as the founders feared. George Washington, for example, warned against having only two political parties: "The alternate domination of one faction over another, sharpened by the spirit of revenge, natural to party dissension, which in different ages and countries has perpetrated the most horrid enormities, is itself a frightful despotism." According to Washington, rival political parties "serve to organize faction, to give it an artificial and extraordinary force; to put, in the place of the delegated will of the nation the will of a party."

John Adams, for his part, considered a two-party system a grave threat to the republic: "[A] division of the republic into two great parties ... is to be dreaded as the greatest political evil."

Early in Washington's presidency, however, two main political parties emerged. Alexander Hamilton led the Federalists; Thomas Jefferson the Democratic Republicans.[34] The political warfare between them was extreme. And neither party lasted long. By the mid-nineteenth century, the party system started taking a form similar to today's.[35] The Democrats and Republicans' dominance began just before Abraham Lincoln (a Republican) won the presidency in 1860. The parties' power ebbed and flowed from there. After the Civil War, it grew as immigrants flooded into the country, creating new constituencies. Then it waned during Franklin Delano Roosevelt's presidency (1933–1945), which saw—with World War Two and the New Deal—atypical uniformity in American politics and governance. Beginning in the 1950s, the Democrats and Republicans solidified their hold on America's two-party political system. Today the duopoly is unrivaled.

That's not to say, however, that third parties never matter. Because competition between the two powerhouses is close—with elections often decided by single-digit differentials—third parties with small constituencies can be consequential. In 1992, for example, independent presidential candidate Ross Perot got 18.9% of the popular vote. Democrat Bill Clinton won the Electoral College, and thus the presidency, with only 43% of the popular vote. Republican George H. W. Bush, for his part, received 37.4% of the popular vote.[36] And in 2000, Green Party candidate Ralph Nader won 2.7% of the popular vote.[37] Republican George W. Bush beat Democrat Al Gore by winning just a few more votes in Florida.

Reflexively partisan interpretations of these elections abound. Democrats assert Clinton would've won even if Perot hadn't run; while Republicans allege that Perot's presence cost Bush Senior the election. And Democrats argue Gore would've won if Nader hadn't run; while Republicans claim that Bush Junior would've won either way. Given the many variables that have an impact on presidential elections, it is, of course, impossible to really know.

Today, third parties still struggle to gain traction or have influence beyond merely being potential spoilers. As Gerald Seib wrote in August 2023 in the *Wall Street Journal*, "even as voters express unhappiness with their political choices, they have become more locked into their partisan preferences and voting patterns. If Democrats today struggle to woo Republicans to their side, and vice versa, is it plausible to think an independent or third-party candidate would have more success? In any case, the winner-take-all nature of the presidential election system, under which no Electoral College votes are rewarded just for coming close to winning a state, makes the task even harder."

Monopolies breed sloppiness. And most Americans have one binary choice—Democrats or Republicans—predetermined by their ideological preference. Thus, as we'll analyze throughout Part Two, the parties are neither disciplined nor coherent. They are, indeed, a mess. While the Democrats still have rational and sober-minded leadership, the party's radical progressive wing is far too influential. The wing's positions in areas like free speech (cancel dissent), law enforcement (defund the police), national defense (a trivial concern), and federal spending (deficits don't matter)—to name a few—are unmoored from empirical reality.

The Republicans, meanwhile, are an unfathomable train wreck. Led by Donald Trump and energized by a band of nihilistic zealots in the House of Representatives, the party stands for little more than causing trouble. Traditional Republican leaders are aghast at what the party has become. Two-time Republican Attorney General William Barr, for example, said, "I think the historic problem we have is that Trump is a demagogue who is turning part of the Republican Party into a howling mob. And they have to start considering that acting just from impulsive anger and fury is not the way to turn things around and it sells our country short." Former federal appellate judge Michael Luttig put it this way: "A political party is a collection and assemblage of individuals who share a set of beliefs and principles and policy views about the United States of America. Today, there is no such shared set of beliefs and values and principles or even policy views within the Republican Party for America."

Utah Senator Mitt Romney (the 2012 Republican presidential nominee) summed up his view simply: "A very large portion of my party really doesn't believe in the Constitution." He's right. And this is a really big deal. America's representative democracy depends on Americans believing in and adhering to the Constitution. Not because it gets everything right. It doesn't. And not because there aren't valid alternative governmental structures. There are. Americans must believe in the Constitution, as enacted, because a central, agreed-upon set of overarching rules is a precondition to a civilized and cohesive society.

More than two centuries after the Constitution set out to "form a more perfect union" and "ensure domestic tranquility" and "promote the general welfare," a large part of one America's two major political parties has cast all this aside.

THE RULE OF LAW

America's Constitution, legislation, and judicial opinions set forth laws on paper. But *respect* for the rule of law—in people's hearts and minds—is the necessary precondition for a legal system to work.

This starts with respecting court orders. In America the courts—not the president or Congress—resolve disputes and, in the process, review and define the Constitution and federal laws. This principle, known as judicial review, is nowhere to be found in the Constitution. It arose in the 1803 case *Marbury v. Madison*.[38] In ruling that the 1789 Judiciary

Act conflicted with the Constitution, Chief Justice John Marshall declared, for the first time, that the judicial branch defines the law: "It is emphatically the province and duty of the judicial department to say what the law is." It's been this way ever since.

It's underappreciated in America how important judicial review is to the rule of law and, in turn, the American polity. This is largely true because the system has worked well and Americans tend to focus disproportionately on what *doesn't* work (an ethos both helpful, in prompting improvements, and harmful, in fomenting discontent). The key is that judicial rulings should be respected and followed. Always. This allows litigants' expectations to be set, disputes to be resolved, decisions to be honored, and people to move on. Respecting the finality of judicial review is especially important when, like today, political passions run high. If there was not a deep and powerful tradition in America of respecting court orders as the last word, disputes would drag on, multiply, and intensify.

Having the power to define the Constitution reposed in the judiciary makes sense. Judges restrain the presidency. They check administrative agencies. And they keep Congress in line. Under the Constitution, moreover, judges sit for life upon good behavior.[39] They don't run for re-election and are therefore politically insulated. Because judges must be nominated by the president and confirmed by a Senate majority, however, political accountability undergirds their selection. Indeed, one of American government's most effective parts is the confirmation process (for judges and executive-branch officials) where moderate and responsible Senators can reject extremist nominees. The result is a judiciary that tends to be more rational and principled than the executive and legislative branches. "The Judiciary," Alexander Hamilton wrote in Federalist No. 78, "has no influence over either the sword or the purse; no direction either of the strength or of the wealth of the society; and can take no active resolution whatever. It may truly be said to have neither FORCE nor WILL, but merely judgment." Compared to the political branches (often a low bar, admittedly), the judiciary, including the Supreme Court, has historically exercised this judgment well.

There have been exceptions, however. First among them: *Dred Scott v. Sandford* (1857),[40] where the Supreme Court ruled (1) that slaves weren't American citizens and therefore weren't entitled to the federal government's protections, and (2) that Congress couldn't ban slavery in federal territory. In *Plessy v. Ferguson* (1896),[41] moreover, the court upheld a Louisiana law authorizing "equal but separate accommodations for the white and colored races." The court held that states' segregation laws didn't violate the 14th Amendment's Equal Protection Clause. In *Lochner v. New York* (1905),[42] the court struck down a New York law limiting the hours bakers could be forced to work. The court ruled the law interfered with parties' freedom of contract, and therefore the 14th Amendment's right to liberty. And in *Korematsu v. United States* (1944)[43] the court upheld the legitimacy of relocation camps for Japanese Americans during World War Two. The court's order led to the forced relocation of more than 120,000 Japanese Americans.

These abominations fundamentally tested the Supreme Court's legitimacy. And this century, the court has tested its legitimacy again. In the process, the justices have jeopardized Americans' continued respect for judicial review and the rule of law. It began with three successive body blows to Democrats. The first landed in late 2000 when the court decided—sharply along partisan lines—the presidential election between Republican George W. Bush and Democrat Al Gore. The result of the election came down to who would win in Florida, where recount officials were using different standards in different voting precincts. The procedural difficulties were immense. In *Bush v. Gore*,[44] the court held five to four that no Constitutional recount could occur in the time remaining to resolve the election. This gave Bush the victory.

Democrats went berserk. In his law-review article, "The Unbearable Wrongness of *Bush v. Gore*," Al Gore's attorney in the dispute (and Harvard law professor) Laurence Tribe emoted: "[T]he Court's failure to grapple with the underlying equal protection issues, or to grasp the breathtaking implications of its equal protection holding (including the inconsistency between that holding and the outcome that it endorsed in Florida itself), evince the almost embarrassing bankruptcy of the rationale that the Court's majority adopted." But the court's underlying legal rationale mattered little. Having unelected judges decide a presidential election—in either direction—was sure to enrage half the country. And the people's distrust of the court was exacerbated as Bush appointed two conservative justices, John Roberts and Samuel Alito, who sent the court's jurisprudence sharply to the right. As liberal justice Stephen Breyer said grimly while reading a dissent from the bench: "It is not often in the law that so few have so quickly changed so much."

Then came the second body blow. In Barack Obama's last year in office, 2016, sitting justice Antonin Scalia (a conservative) passed away. Obama nominated centrist federal appellate judge Merrick Garland to replace Scalia. But the Republican-controlled Senate refused to hold confirmation hearings. Led by the Senate Majority Leader from Kentucky, Mitch McConnell, Republicans asserted that it was up to the Senate majority—alone—to decide whether to consider the president's nomination. "The president nominates. The Senate confirms. The American people should have a voice, not this lame duck president out the door," McConnell said. "All we are doing is following *the long-standing tradition of not fulfilling a nomination in the middle of a presidential year.*" (Author's emphasis—remember those words.) This refusal to confirm Garland betrayed Republicans' core Constitutional responsibilities: the presidential prerogative to appoint justices isn't void merely because it's an election year. And it worked. Donald Trump, a Republican, was elected president several months later. And Trump, in turn, quickly nominated conservative justice Neil Gorsuch, who McConnell and Senate Republicans giddily confirmed.

Democrats seethed. And then things got worse. Conservative-leaning Justice Anthony Kennedy resigned and Trump nominated federal appellate judge Brett Kavanaugh, a more conservative judge than Kennedy in key areas (including abortion). At Kavanaugh's confirmation hearing,

Democrats gave center stage to Christine Blasey Ford, who accused Kavanaugh of sexually assaulting her when they were teenagers, thirty years earlier. The Senate confirmed Kavanaugh 50–48.[45] While Kavanaugh's confirmation hearing was an unfortunate spectacle, his appointment was—ironically—the least controversial Republican appointment this century: Justice Kennedy resigned and Trump, the duly elected president, filled his seat in the normal way.

Then came the decisive blow. Sitting justice Ruth Bader Ginsburg (a liberal) passed away in 2020, just a few months before the presidential election. Ginsburg was well into her eighties and had been encouraged to resign several years earlier during President Obama's first term, when the Democrats controlled the Senate. She refused. And Senate Republicans did what Senate Republicans do: they flip-flopped. Confirming a justice during a presidential election year suddenly wasn't a problem. And in strode another conservative justice, Amy Coney Barrett, to replace Ginsburg.

Ginsburg was an American hero who broadened legal rights and protections for all Americans as both an advocate and a judge. She will rightfully retain a special place in the long history of American law. But her refusal to resign in her eighties cost Democrats a highly consequential seat on the court. And in an historic irony—one that few on the left will admit in public—this champion of women's rights directly cost American women the Constitutional right to an abortion. (Justice Breyer learned this lesson and resigned, at 83, when President Biden had a Democratic Senate majority in 2022.)

Thus, three instances of happenstance—*Bush v. Gore*, McConnell's betrayal, and Ginsburg's refusal—placed four new conservative justices on the nine-person court. Consider a simple counter-history: if Al Gore had won a few more votes in Florida, if Scalia had died a few months earlier, and if Ginsburg had retired a few years earlier, then so much would have been so different. Today the court would have seven liberals dominating its jurisprudence rather than three being marginalized.

Because the power of judicial review is so awesome, these events will reverberate for decades. For better or for worse, America's Supreme Court shapes the contours of the separation of powers, federalism, free speech, abortion, gun rights, voting rights, criminal justice, environmental regulations, and so much more.

The court's new conservative super-majority should have recognized that maintaining respect for the rule of law and judicial review requires the American people's broad acceptance. Given how they assumed their majority—and the fragility of a polity riven by polarization—the conservatives should have been modest and measured with their jurisprudence. They should have trodden carefully and respectfully. They should have moved slowly.

Instead, they rocked the system to its core.

In May 2022, the court overruled *Roe v. Wade*.[46] A bare majority of five conservative justices shattered a fifty-year-old precedent on abortion—perhaps the most divisive topic in American politics. The worst part of it all is that they didn't have to. The court could have simply held that the Mississippi law at issue, which bans abortion after fifteen weeks, was Constitutional and left it there. Restricting the time for protecting abortions to fifteen weeks would have sharply reduced abortion rights in states throughout the country. But that huge victory wasn't enough.

And they didn't stop there. The very same week, the conservative justices struck down a New York gun regulation, construing the 2nd Amendment to give Americans the broad right to carry firearms in public.[47] Fresh off the aggressive expansion of federalism with abortion, sending the issue to the states, the conservative justices lurched in the opposite direction and imposed their preferences on guns nationwide—right in the middle of a national crisis of gun deaths. Again, they didn't have to. They could have simply declined to hear the case.

Respect for judicial review and the finality of court decisions is central to the rule of law. And Americans of all stripes still do respect court orders. But this won't last if the court sacrifices its long-term legitimacy to satisfy short-term judicial cravings. By electing to gratuitously overturn *Roe* and expand the 2nd Amendment, the court's conservatives undermined its essential place in America's Constitutional constellation. A very small number of lawyers dressed in robes leaned deep into the darkest corners of American tribalism and polarization and forced *all* Americans to toe *their* line. They did so at precisely the wrong time. In precisely the wrong way. And not because they had to—but simply because they could.

CAPITALISM

Another essential tradition of the American experiment is capitalism. A market-based economy with strong privacy rights is a core feature of how America works.

It's been this way from the outset. Alexander Hamilton was the nation's first Treasury Secretary. According to the *New York Times'* columnist David Brooks, Hamilton "forged the modern financial and economic systems that are the basis for American might today." When Hamilton took the reins at the Treasury the American economy was teetering on the ragged edge of post-war insolvency. He nationalized the debt, which bound the states together economically, and created capital markets that have supported American prosperity ever since. Hamilton revered the energy and ingenuity in a vibrant, open-market economy. As he observed: "Every new scene, which is opened to the busy nature of man to rouse and exert itself, is the addition of a new energy to the general stock of effort."

It has long been fashionable to bash capitalism as the root of America's problems. Even great American heroes have taken their turn. The Reverend Martin Luther King Jr., for example, said that with capitalism, "a small privileged few are rich beyond conscience, and almost all others are doomed to be poor at some level. That's the way the system works. And since we know that the system will not change the rules, we are going to have to change the system." The deaf and blind author Helen Keller put it this way: "The country is governed for the richest, for the corporations, the bankers, the land speculators, and for the exploiters of labor. The majority of mankind are working people. So long as their fair demands—the ownership and control of their livelihoods—are set at naught, we can have neither men's rights nor women's rights. The majority of mankind is ground down by industrial oppression in order that the small remnant may live in ease." Civil-rights activist Malcom X was even less subtle: "You show me a capitalist, and I'll show you a bloodsucker."

While these and other critics often overstate the case, capitalism isn't without flaws. Slavery, of course, saw white American men buying, selling, and exploiting Black slaves. According to author Matthew Desmond, "In order to understand the brutality of American capitalism, you have to start on the plantation." Slavery was the American South's economic engine from before the founding through the Civil War. Capitalist exploitation, moreover, continued long past the end of slavery. Excessive hours, terrible conditions, low wages, and even child labor were all rampant before the mid-twentieth century, when important labor laws protecting workers emerged.[48] And while worker protections for Americans are now robust, American consumers still purchase goods from countries far less concerned with labor conditions and employee rights.[49]

While many of American capitalism's negatives have softened with time (at least domestically), two huge scourges remain. The first is inequality. Capitalism helps the rich get richer. As we'll see in Chapter 8, the gap between America's ultra-rich and lower class is jaw-dropping. This extreme inequality causes deep anger and resentment within America's middle and lower classes.

Some amount of inequality, however, is a good thing. Ambitious and hard-working people should be motivated to get ahead and rewarded for their success. Allowing reasonable amounts of inequality is better than rigidly enforcing equal outcomes. But America's *excessive* level of inequality poisons the body politic. Hundreds of billionaires (some with a net worth well above $100 billion)[50] shouldn't coexist with millions of people struggling to find food and shelter.[51]

American capitalism's second big negative is environmental harm. Capitalism has an inherent trade-off: it brings an abundance of goods to the market, but it degrades the environment in the process.[52] Large companies cut down trees to make paper; drill to excavate oil; pollute the air to deliver packages; warm the planet as a result of farming cattle; create non-biodegradable plastic to package merchandise; contaminate water to manufacture goods. And so on. While the amount of this harm varies depending on the size of the economy, the strength of regulations, and the effectiveness of countervailing innovations, there's no escaping the basic fact that capitalism harms the environment. As we'll examine in Chapter 8, America can do far better in limiting this harm.

Capitalism's negatives are, indeed, significant. But they are emphatically outweighed by its positives. A market-based economy motivates people to innovate and produce helpful products and services far more effectively than a command-based system. Incentives matter. And many (though not all) people will be more productive if they're rewarded disproportionately for their efforts. Almost all Americans have gained from ambitious and energetic people who are rewarded for building things profitably—i.e., the way people want them.

Sure, people sometimes want things they shouldn't, like cheap French fries, fancy casinos, harsh cigarettes, and addictive social-media platforms. But providing people with more choices, even if some are harmful, is far better than miring them in stasis. Private companies' innovations have, on balance, dramatically increased human flourishing. Handheld computers supercharge numerous walks of life; the internet makes the world's information accessible; medicine improves and prolongs human life; airplanes make global travel a widespread reality; communication systems connect billions of people; industrial food production and distribution reduce hunger; architecture and engineering provide places for people to work and play. And so on.

Moreover, while the fruits of capitalism are distributed unevenly, they nonetheless broadly enhance daily life for most Americans. For example, as Harvard professor Steven Pinker explained in his book *Enlightenment Now*, in 2011 almost all "American households below the poverty line had electricity, running water, flush toilets, a refrigerator, a stove, and a color TV. (A century and a half before, the Rothschilds, Astors, and Vanderbilts had none of these things.)"

Many critics assert that the biggest problems with American capitalism are inherent in capitalism itself. This is false. The *extent* of American capitalism's biggest flaws is unnecessary. Inequality could be addressed through the tax system while maintaining free markets. While a wealth tax, for example, would be difficult to administer, it could nonetheless materially reduce excessive inequality. Likewise, better regulations would alleviate substantial damage to the environment. A cap-and-trade system, for example, would reduce harmful emissions. While some amount of inequality and environmental harm is inherent in capitalism, the depths of these problems are flaws in the *American version* of capitalism—not capitalism itself.

Underlying many of capitalism's most impassioned critiques is a pathology that pervades the American polity:

taking things for granted. Echoing detractors of American government, critics of American capitalism often thoroughly enjoy the fruits of the system while bashing its flaws. They write scathing critiques on their sophisticated laptops, in books published by large conglomerates, while sipping fancy Starbucks lattes, pausing to tweet to a globally integrated audience from their hand-held supercomputers, all while draped in chic clothing made by huge corporations leveraging global supply chains. The irony is rich: many of American capitalism's biggest critics reap huge rewards from the system.

Data from around the world confirm capitalism's positive net impact on humanity. Economic growth rooted in free markets and liberalized trade—two core features of capitalism—has lifted over a billion people out of poverty since the late twentieth century.[53] The Department for International Development's 2008 report *Growth: Building Jobs and Prosperity in Developing Countries* cites several examples of this miraculous progress:

- "China alone has lifted over 450 million people out of poverty since 1979. Evidence shows that rapid economic growth between 1985 and 2001 was crucial to this enormous reduction in poverty."
- "India has seen significant falls in poverty since the 1980s, rates that accelerated into the 1990s. This has been strongly related to India's impressive growth record over this period."
- "Mozambique illustrates the rapid reduction in poverty associated with growth over a shorter period. Between 1996 and 2002, the economy grew by 62 percent and the

proportion of people living in poverty declined from 69 percent to 54 percent."

- "The reduction in poverty was particularly spectacular in Vietnam, where poverty fell by 7.8 percent a year between 1993 and 2002, halving the poverty rate from 58 percent to 29 percent."
- "Other countries with impressive reductions over this period include El Salvador, Ghana, India, Tunisia and Uganda, each with declines in the poverty rate of between three and six percent a year."

In stark contrast, those few countries that haven't joined the global capitalist system lag far behind. And their people struggle accordingly. South Korea and North Korea—two nations of Korean people—make a striking comparison. The former's real GDP per capita in 2022 was $36,101; the latter's was $1,720.[54] A night-time image from outer space shows South Korea brightly lit up by the modern abundance provided by its free-market economy. North Korea, meanwhile, lies in darkness as its people suffer from poverty, malnutrition, and disease, deprived of modern innovations that most of the world now enjoys.

Notwithstanding its many flaws—and its even greater number of critics—capitalism does a lot more good than harm. It's a fundamental part of how America works ... and why it has worked well.

AMERICA HAS WORKED
America has, indeed, worked well. Rooted in human history's lessons and the Enlightenment's ideals, America's

Constitutional principles and essential traditions have contributed to a dramatic increase in human flourishing. The separation of powers has prevented undue concentrations of authority and influence. Local governments have thrived in the federalist system. The freedom of speech and rule of law have remained strong compared to most nations. America has, moreover, grown more inclusive as rights have steadily spread across the population. The judiciary is still respected as the last word on the Constitution. And capitalism has generated unimagined prosperity: the tiny new nation with under one percent of the world's population rose eventually to produce, at its peak, 40 percent of the world's GDP.[55]

The American-led international order has also seen huge improvements globally—improvements that closely track America's own positive trajectory. Human beings fight in wars (in America as elsewhere) much less frequently than they used to.[56] Extreme poverty has plummeted from about 90 percent of the world's population to about 10 percent.[57] Literacy has skyrocketed from about 15 percent of the world's population to more than 85 percent.[58] Longevity has increased from about 30 years to about 70 years, and to about 80 years in the developed world.[59] In key measure after key measure, human flourishing has increased globally since America's founding. America doesn't deserve all the credit for these improvements, of course, but it has undoubtedly played a vital role in bringing them about.

America's progress hasn't been linear, to be sure. American sins have decreased over time, but have never disappeared. And if one compares America to hypothetical nations that never existed (a common exercise), then its light dramatically dims. America's reality fails miserably compared to the imagination's utopias. But on balance and in practice, the American experiment has been a success by any rational historical standard.

Around the turn of the twenty-first century, however, the trend line started reversing. This didn't begin instantaneously on January 1, 2000. Not everything was great before then; not everything is terrible now. And the trajectory may again return to being positive. But around this time, as the internet began its intrusion into daily life, the causes of America's decline started to take hold. A national addiction to social media, rampant tribalism, and America's flawed political structure all combined to turbocharge irrationality and, in turn, degrade and destabilize the body politic.

In ways both big and small, twenty-first-century America has stopped working.

PART TWO

AND WHY IT DOESN'T

"Within the character of the citizen, lies the welfare of the nation"

Marcus Tullius Cicero

American democracy is backsliding in the twenty-first century. The root cause is the combination of three factors. First, political tribalism that enflames age-old cognitive biases. Second, brand-new social-media platforms that transform how people publish, consume, and process information. And third, long-entrenched structural deficiencies, like the two-party duopoly, that distort the US political system.

The combination of these three components is a flywheel spinning faster and faster every day. Social media exacerbates tribalism by feeding users confirmatory and incendiary political news. The two-party political system compounds the resulting irrationality by pitting two juggernauts against each other in a bitter, all-consuming rivalry that stifles and deforms the marketplace of ideas. The polarized political debate, in turn, turbocharges over-stimulated tribal biases with partisan falsehoods (e.g., Trump colluded with Russia to hack the DNC's email servers), gross caricatures (e.g., Hillary Clinton is a crooked felon), and abhorrent stupidities (e.g., Barack Obama was born in Kenya).

And so the flywheel spins.

This throbbing frenzy erodes respect for the Constitutional principles and essential traditions of American democracy examined in Part One—a respect that is necessary for them to function. Indeed, these principles and traditions aren't laws of physics; they are rules for structuring society that require good faith, compromise, and broad consent to work. And they will eventually disintegrate if the American people continue to ignore them while fixating instead on short-term political battles. A nation is, indeed, little more than the hearts and minds of its people. And a big part of why America isn't working is because Americans have stopped caring about how it's supposed to work.

Part Two analyzes the destructive combination of tribalism, social media, and the US political system (Chapter 6); examines the corresponding political dysfunction (Chapter 7); dissects significant resulting public-policy failures (Chapter 8); assesses the two biggest threats to American democracy (Chapter 9); and considers America's future (Chapter 10).

6

Tribalism, Social Media, and Political Structure

"There are two kinds of people in the world: those who divide the world into two kinds of people, and those who don't"
Robert Benchley

The root cause of America's twenty-first-century decline is the combination of (1) tribalism, (2) social media, and (3) a malformed political structure.

(1) TRIBALISM

Humans lived in tribes for most of our history. The bonds of tribalism are thus deeply hardwired into the human psyche. Tribalism makes us loyal to and biased in favor of fellow members of our own tribe. In the process, it distorts our thinking, overriding facts and data. And it makes us biased against outsiders who we dislike and perceive to be a threat.

This makes some sense. For a very long period, human survival depended on being tribal. The more loyal and organized the tribe, the more effective it would be at fending off threats from animals and rival clans. Yale law professor Amy Chua highlighted the power of tribalism in her book *Political Tribes: Group Instinct and the Fate of Nations*: "Humans, like other primates, are tribal animals. We need to belong to groups, which is why we love clubs and teams. Once people connect with a group, their identities can become powerfully bound to it. They will seek to benefit members of their group even when they gain nothing personally. They will penalize outsiders, seemingly gratuitously. They will sacrifice, and even kill and die, for their group."

America's two big political tribes are liberals and conservatives. Two key indicators reveal how dramatically the fault-line between them divides the country. First, Americans struggle even to discuss politics with people from the opposing tribe. As Pew Research reported in November 2019, "At a time when the country's polarizing politics and public discourse are dividing many Americans, close to half of all U.S. adults acknowledge that they have stopped discussing political and election news with someone ... In total, 45% of the nation's adults say they have stopped talking about political and election news with someone as a result of something they said, either in person or online."

Second, Americans now rarely marry across the political divide. According to Pew Research, even religious differences are now less of a barrier to marriage: "Sizable minorities of married people are members of a different religious group than their partner, but marriages and partnerships across political party lines are relatively rare. About four-in-ten Americans who have married since 2010 (39%) have a spouse who is in a different religious group, compared with only 19% of those who wed before 1960 … When it comes to politics, a 2016 Pew Research Center survey found 77% of both Republicans and Democrats who were married or living with a partner said their spouse or partner was in the same party."[60]

The essence of tribalism is to be biased in favor of your tribe and against another tribe. To understand tribalism you must therefore understand cognitive biases, which are systemic mental processes that simplify and distort people's observations and experiences. Most people are familiar with cognitive biases and see them in numerous everyday contexts. Sporting events are a great example, where fans rabidly cheer for their team and, in the process, consistently interpret events (like close calls from the referee) inaccurately in favor of their team (or tribe).

But three underappreciated aspects of cognitive biases make them much more powerful than is commonly understood. First, most people don't think *they're* biased; it's *other people* who are afflicted. The brain tricks us into thinking that we're seeing things accurately when we aren't. This helps explain why a variety of contradictory political views from different people are all expressed with great confidence, even though—by definition—only one view can be correct.

As writer Oliver Burkeman has explained, this "bias blind spot" lies behind the famous "better-than-average effect, or Lake Wobegon effect, whereby the majority of people think they're above average on any number of measures— their driving skills, their popularity, the quality of their relationship—when clearly they can't all be right." The bias blind spot "also applies to bias," Burkeman continued. "In other words, we're convinced that we're better than most at not falling victim to bias."

Second, most people don't understand how incredibly potent cognitive biases are. Biases aren't merely quirky defects that impair thinking at the margins. Nor are biases limited to discrete areas like sports and politics. Bias is, rather, a powerful force that fundamentally deforms and degrades human thinking across a variety of subjects.

Finally, people of all intelligence levels are equally affected by bias. Indeed, smarter people are often the most biased of all. This concept even has a name: "the smart idiot effect." Better-educated Republicans, for example, tend to have stronger views denying climate change than their less-well-educated counterparts.[61] This counterintuitive phenomenon occurs because smart people are better at interpreting (or twisting) new information to fit their pre-existing world-view. Indeed, intelligent people often make political polarization worse. As Yale professor Dan Kahan explains, "[T]he capacities associated with science literacy can actually impede public recognition of the best available evidence and deepen pernicious forms of cultural polarization." University of Toronto professor Keith Stanovich's research on "myside bias" (confirmation bias in the political realm) also shows how biases affect people irrespective of intelligence. "Research across a wide variety of myside bias paradigms has revealed a somewhat surprising finding regarding individual differences. The magnitude of the myside bias shows very little relation to intelligence."

In sum: cognitive biases are really powerful, affect everyone (including you and me, dear reader), and hide themselves so that we don't think we're biased at all. That's a potent combination. And in America, 335 million people wake up every day with some version of this combination at work.

THE NARRATIVE FALLACY

Several specific biases fuel political tribalism. The narrative fallacy, for example, is the ubiquitous tendency in humans to over-simplify things and create coherent—yet false—narratives. We take small sets of discrete facts and construct broad and elaborate stories. In the process, we connect the dots, or fill in the blanks, with fiction. It makes sense that this bias would exist: the world is far too large and complicated to fully process everything around us. As Nobel Prize-winning psychologist Daniel Kahneman explains, the narrative fallacy creates misimpressions because "the confidence that individuals have in their beliefs depends mostly on the quality of the story they can tell about what they see, even if they see little."

Two recent examples illustrate the narrative fallacy's power and prevalence in US politics. The first is the widespread belief among Republicans in the 2010s that then-President Barack Obama was born outside the US (in Kenya) and was therefore Constitutionally ineligible to be president. The evidence was scant: Obama is African American. His father was from Kenya. His last name has African roots. And, well, that's about it. Yet the narrative was sweeping: Obama really had been born in Kenya (not Hawaii as he claimed); he had manufactured a fake birth certificate; and he had perpetrated a multi-decade scam—culminating in a Constitutional fraud upon the American people—by lying about his birthplace.

Donald Trump was the tribal ringleader trumpeting the fallacious "birther" narrative. "I have people that have been studying [Obama's birth certificate] and they cannot believe what they're finding," he said in 2011. "I would like to have him show his birth certificate, and can I be honest with you, I hope he can. Because if he can't, if he can't, if he wasn't born in this country, which is a real possibility ... then he has pulled one of the great cons in the history of politics." Tens of millions of Republicans believed this nonsense for years.

The second example of the narrative fallacy involved the widespread belief among Democrats that Donald Trump co-ordinated with Russian President Vladimir Putin in 2016 to hack into the Democratic National Committee's email servers. Again, the evidence was scant: Trump had said nice things about Putin. Russia hacked the DNC. Many thought the hack gave Trump the 2016 election win over Hillary Clinton. And, well, that's about it. Yet again, the narrative was sweeping: Trump and Putin, either directly or through subordinates, colluded in cyberspace to hack into the DNC's computer network and steal embarrassing DNC emails. Then the clandestine collaborators provided the goods to website WikiLeaks just weeks before the election—giving Trump his illicit victory. A huge percentage of Democrats, including many party leaders, jumped on the tribal bandwagon. Obama's CIA Director John Brennan, for example, said in August 2018 that "Mr. Trump's claims of no collusion [with Russia] are, in a word, hogwash."

Donald Trump is capable of a lot of things. And he would do a lot of other things if he could. But the idea that he was in cahoots with Putin to hack into the DNC was always absurd. Russia has long had active global cybersecurity operations. There was no reason for them to involve Trump. Was he going to provide them with new and innovative cyber-hacking techniques? Or DNC staffer email usernames and passwords? Bringing Trump and his disorganized, rag-tag campaign into Russia's sophisticated cyber operations would only have increased the odds that Russia's hack would be stymied beforehand or uncovered afterwards. Trump's positive statements about Putin during (and after) the campaign were concerning, to be sure. But the facts never supported the fallacious narrative that Trump helped perpetrate the DNC hack.

AVAILABILITY BIAS

Another bias that's prevalent in US politics is the availability bias. This bias causes people to over-emphasize information that's recalled easily—even if that information is not useful or important. Information that's easy to recall—that's readily available—is often low quality and misleading. As Harvard psychologist Steven Pinker explains: "Our assessment of risk and danger is driven by available episodes from memory, not representative data. If you ask people if we are living in an increasingly dangerous or increasingly safe environment, they will think of the latest terrorist attack and conclude that life has been getting more dangerous—rather than going to FBI data on violent crime, which in fact has shown a decline over 25 years."

Like other biases, the availability bias's power and consequences are underestimated. Often dramatically. Pinker again:

> The availability bias may affect the fate of the planet. Several eminent climate scientists, having crunched the numbers, warn that 'there is no credible path to climate stabilization that does not include a substantial role for nuclear power'. Nuclear power is the safest form of energy humanity has ever used. Mining accidents, hydroelectric dam failures, natural gas explosions, and oil train crashes all kill people, sometimes in large numbers, and smoke from burning coal kills them in enormous numbers, more than half a million per year. Yet nuclear power has stalled for decades in the United States and is being pushed back in Europe, often replaced by dirty and dangerous coal. In large part the opposition is driven by memories of three accidents: Three Mile Island in 1979, which killed no one; Fukushima in 2011, which killed one worker years later (the other deaths were caused by the tsunami and from a panicked evacuation); and the Soviet-bungled Chernobyl in 1986, which killed 31 in the accident and perhaps several thousand from cancer, around the same number killed by coal emissions every day.

A related concept is an availability cascade.[62] This self-reinforcing process occurs when a news topic gets significant coverage and online discussion, which increases its availability to news consumers. This, in turn, makes consumers more likely to believe its veracity and restate it publicly, triggering still more stories and discussion. This can lead to large-scale and self-perpetuating media cycles that dramatically affect public discourse—even when the story is false.

Returning to the "birther" falsehood, one reason so many Republicans believed Obama was born in Kenya was because so many people were talking about it. And the fact that so many people were talking about the controversy made *even more* people talk about it. It was everywhere. For years. This kept the crackpot narrative uppermost in the minds of millions of people, giving it a legitimacy it didn't deserve.

The same thing was true with Trump and Russia. One reason so many people believed that Trump colluded with Putin to hack into the DNC's email servers is because that story—and an entire industry of related innuendo—was pounded into them on television, radio, online, and in print. Day after day after day. The bombardment made people think it was true even though the evidence was missing.

David Hume once said, "A wise man proportions his belief to the evidence." In twenty-first-century America, beliefs are often proportioned to how viral a narrative gets— irrespective of the evidence.

CONFIRMATION BIAS
The biggest bias of all in American politics is confirmation bias, which courses through the bloodstream of the body politic. This bias is fundamental to the human psyche, which has a powerful propensity to construe new information as consistent with pre-existing beliefs.

Confirmation bias has two main parts. The first is to amplify and celebrate new information that fits with one's ideological preference. If the GDP rises when your party is in power, this proves their economic policies work. The second is to diminish and ignore new information that conflicts with one's ideological preference. If the GDP rises when the *other* party is in office, however, then broad economic trends— or the lagging effects of the predecessor administration's policies—are at work.

As Harvard professor Thomas Patterson explains, "Confirmation bias causes us to respond selectively to information in a way that reinforces what we want to believe." And again, as with other biases, people don't think they're affected by confirmation bias when, in reality, they are. As Annie Duke wrote in *Thinking in Bets*, "We might think of ourselves as open-minded and capable of updating our beliefs based on new information, but the research conclusively shows otherwise. Instead of altering our beliefs to fit new information, we do the opposite, altering our interpretation of that information to fit our beliefs."

Carol Tavris and Elliot Aronson in their book *Mistakes Were Made (But Not by Me)* highlight how confirmation bias is so powerful that even consuming quality information *at odds* with your political views "can make you all the more convinced you are right. In one experiment, researchers selected people who either favored or opposed capital punishment and asked them to read two scholarly, well-documented articles on the emotionally charged issue of whether the death penalty deters violent crimes. One article concluded that it did; the other that it didn't." Tavris and Aronson predicted "that the readers would find a way to distort the two articles. They would find reasons to clasp the confirming article to their bosoms, hailing it as a highly competent piece of work. And they would be supercritical of the disconfirming article, finding minor flaws and magnifying them into major reasons why they need not be influenced by it. This is precisely what happened. Not only did each side discredit the other's arguments; each side became even more committed to its own."

Perhaps the most surprising effect of confirmation bias in politics is the degree to which people refuse to change their minds even when their tribal theories are conclusively rejected—ruled out, destroyed, blown to smithereens—by the facts. For example, President Obama produced his birth certificate in 2011. It proved he was born in Hawaii, as he had said all along. Yet as reported by NPR, well into 2016 "[t]he birther issue still [held] considerable traction with a large swath of Republican voters ... [as] 41 percent surveyed disagreed with the statement, 'Barack Obama was born in the United States.' An additional 31 percent of Republicans neither agreed nor disagreed with the statement and only a quarter of Republicans surveyed believed Obama was born in the U.S." Even Donald Trump—to whom concession is the ultimate sin—admitted that he had been peddling a scam: "President Obama was born in the United States. Period," Trump said. "Now, we want to get back to making America strong and great again."

And in a startling display of confirmation bias from the other side of the tribal divide, many Democrats *still* argue that Trump colluded with Russia. This belief persists even after Special Counsel Robert Mueller's unambiguous determination to the contrary after an exhaustive multi-year investigation: "The investigation did not establish that members of the Trump Campaign conspired or co-ordinated with the Russian government in its election interference activities." According to these Democrats, two incidents prove that Trump's campaign really did collude with Russia after all. The first was a June 2016 meeting at Trump Tower between Trump campaign officials and a Russian lawyer who promised to provide damaging evidence about Hillary Clinton. Emails show music promoter Rob Goldstone arranging the meeting with Donald Trump Jr., telling him that "the crown prosecutor of Russia" had offered "to provide the Trump campaign with some official documents and information that would incriminate Hillary and her dealings with Russia and would be very useful to your father." Goldstone added: "This is obviously very high level and sensitive information but is part of Russia and its government's support for Mr. Trump." Trump Jr. replied: "If it's what you say, I love it, especially later in the summer."

The meeting proved to be fruitless: the Russian had nothing valuable to offer Trump's campaign, about Hillary or otherwise.[63] But it was highly improper. Trump Jr. should have rejected Goldstone's outreach. Yet the meeting was nonetheless *exculpating* evidence regarding Trump-Russian collusion. If Trump's campaign really was in the middle of an elaborate cyber-espionage scheme with Russia to sabotage the Clinton campaign, then the two colluding parties wouldn't have been arranging introductory meetings via email through random intermediaries. They'd be midstream in their secret communications, plotting their next move.

The second supposed piece of evidence substantiating the Democrats' charge of Russian collusion is Trump's then-campaign manager Paul Manafort providing his client, a

Russian oligarch, internal campaign polling data. This, too, was improper. But it was also inconsequential.

Just compare these two trivialities, which later came to light, to the initial allegations: hosting a futile meeting at Trump Tower and sharing the results of a poll are stunningly innocuous compared to perpetrating the DNC cyber hack, a serious felony that may have changed the presidential election's outcome. Ultimately, some Democrats did admit they were wrong. John Brennan, for example, conceded, "I don't know if I received bad information, but I think I suspected there was more than there actually was ... I am relieved that it's been determined there was not a criminal conspiracy with the Russian government over our election." But most stuck to their guns despite the facts.

When confronted with disconfirming evidence, it's better to slow down and give it fair consideration. After noting that "most people early achieve and later intensify a tendency to process new and disconfirming information so that any original conclusion remains intact," investor Charlie Munger celebrated a far better approach. Charles Darwin, by contrast, "always gave priority attention to evidence tending to disconfirm whatever cherished and hard-won theory he already had." This approach of seeking out and considering disconfirming evidence is rare. But it has a virtue that everyone should appreciate: it makes one's thinking far more accurate.

When people look at political questions through a biased tribal lens, they apply their own internal, subjective gloss to the world. This distorts empirical reality, which is completely independent from such subjective mental processing. The main problem with tribal thinking is that it's inaccurate, wrong, mistaken—irrespective of what tribe it comes from. *By definition.* A tribal lens is counterproductive if one's goal is to accurately interpret the world. If your tribe is right about something, then the lens is superfluous. If your tribe is wrong, then the lens is distortive.

Comedian Stephen Colbert may be right about some things (and quite funny to boot), but he was very wrong when he famously said, "Reality has a well-known liberal bias." It doesn't. The empirical world is not liberal or conservative. Sometimes the right answer happens to be liberal; sometimes it happens to be conservative; and sometimes it has no home on either side of the rigid ideological divide. The world unfolds according to the laws of nature and science. Leaves don't rustle in the wind differently depending on which party controls the presidency. Waves don't pound the shore harder when it's an election year. Economic cycles don't suddenly reverse if the minority gains a majority in the legislature. And political policies, events, and scandals don't conform to the knee-jerk perceptions of distant observers.

While politicians and political operatives have incentives to distort the truth, the citizen's goal should be straightforward: to strive to make sense of the world accurately. The alternative is to be wrong, and why would that be better? The comforts of tribalism make conforming to one's group satisfying and protective. But it's far better to be accurate and independent than wrong and tribal. As Frederick Douglass put it, "I prefer to be true to myself, even at the hazard of incurring the ridicule of others, rather than to be false, and to incur my own abhorrence."

Indeed, tribal misjudgment is more than merely an interesting psychological topic or stimulating academic question. Imposing on the world an ideology ridden with mistaken conclusions never goes well—especially in a representative democracy where public opinion often dictates public policy. A government's intellectual premises must be sound for it to work well. And as we'll see in Chapter 9, tribalism in America has contributed to numerous significant public-policy failures.

America's founders understood the dangers of bias and tribalism. America's Constitutional framework is designed to dilute the potency of factions, or political tribes, through the separation of powers and federalism. The 1st Amendment prevents a dominant tribe from silencing weaker clans. And representative democracy, as opposed to direct democracy, insulates the government from popular, bias-driven hysterias. Little did the founders know, however, that just over two hundred years after they enacted the Constitution, millions of connected computing machines harnessing and multiplying the world's information would make tribalism a whole lot worse.

(2) SOCIAL MEDIA

These connected computing machines are, of course, the internet. While tribalism has always caused irrationality in American politics, the internet's growing dominance in the twenty-first century has dramatically compounded the problem.

The internet is the culmination of centuries of evolution of communications technology. For millennia, humans communicated primarily through spoken words and gestures and primitive symbols and depictions. Moveable type wasn't invented until about AD1005, in China.[64] Johannes Gutenberg's printing press arrived a few hundred years later,[65] and books eventually became a central part of human life. Mass-printed pamphlets and newspapers appeared, too, and played a major role in early American politics—galvanizing support for the American Revolution, and, with the Federalist Papers, explaining the new Constitution.

In the early twentieth century came the radio, a revolutionary innovation that broadcast audio into the home. Americans listened to Babe Ruth play baseball and President Franklin Delano Roosevelt give "fireside chats." Television soon followed. By the 1990s, there was a robust ecosystem of books, newspapers, magazines, television shows, and radio programs informing and entertaining most Americans.

These twentieth-century innovations were ground-breaking. But the internet's arrival late in the twentieth century was truly revolutionary. Science fiction came true: a system of connected computers allowed most of the world's digital information to travel instantaneously around the globe in response to people simply clicking buttons on screens.

This transformation in communication has already had a profound impact on human cognition. Our brain has evolved over millions of years to process information primarily about local matters that affect us directly. Humans communicated face to face with fellow members of their tribe. They hunted. They gathered. They drew cave drawings. The brain was wired to grapple with phenomena that could be felt with the hands and seen with the eyes. Then the explosion came: within a few hundred years, humans went from communicating primitively to reading the printing press's early texts, to listening to the radio and watching television, to surfing the web's early sites, to the present day, when millions practically inhale social-media feeds of information from all over the world, manipulated by algorithms.

This disconnect between how humans evolved to process information and how we now process information leaves us vulnerable to exploitative technologies. The single biggest problem is social media, which is scientifically engineered to exploit users' cognitive biases.

Social-media platforms allow people to connect with friends and exchange information within their own personalized online social networks. They emerged in the late 90s and early 2000s. Early social-media sites like Friendster and Myspace began the trend. But Facebook, founded in 2003 (as Facemash) by Harvard student Mark Zuckerberg, soon outpaced these early networks. Other successful sites followed, including LinkedIn (for professional networking), Twitter[66] (for short-form posting), Instagram (for pictures), Snapchat (for ephemeral messaging), YouTube (for videos), and TikTok (for short-form videos). These companies all feverishly pursue the same objective: to attract more eyeballs and increase user engagement, measured by clicks, in order to produce more advertising revenue.

Social media has become dominant in American life. Pew Research explained in April 2021 that, "Today around seven-in-ten Americans use social media to connect with one another, engage with news content, share information and entertain themselves ... For many users, social media is part of their daily routine. Seven-in-ten Facebook users—and around six-in-ten Instagram and Snapchat users—visit these sites at least once a day."

Most Americans think social media is harmful. According to Pew Research in October 2020, "About two-thirds of Americans (64%) say social media have a mostly negative effect on the way things are going in the country today ... Just one-in-ten Americans say social media sites have a mostly positive effect on the way things are going." Pew Research, moreover, found that Americans have deep concerns about social media's impact on political discourse: "Those who have a negative view of the impact of social media mention, in particular, misinformation and the hate and harassment they see on social media. They also have concerns about users believing everything they see or read—or not being sure about what to believe. Additionally, they bemoan social media's role in fomenting partisanship and polarization, the creation of echo chambers, and the perception that these platforms oppose President Donald Trump and conservatives."

These concerns are valid. And their root cause is social media's predominant role in exacerbating political bias and tribalism. It does so in several ways. First, social-media algorithms feed users the content they are most likely to consume based on their previous activity. Social-media feeds are thus confirmation-bias machines: a steady stream of like-minded stories and sources is fed to users, reconfirming their existing worldviews. Social-media feeds consisting primarily of sources from a narrow perspective—as is common—place users into ideologically rigid echo chambers. This, in turn, tends to decrease empathy for opposing views and increase polarization.[67, 68] A main reason the "other" tribe seems so bananas is because it consumes a totally different set of facts and brand of analysis every day on social media.

Second, social-media platforms generate vast quantities of misinformation.[69] There are few checks on the information that is disseminated. Individual users are free to publish their thoughts and share others' content—irrespective of accuracy—on their networks. The narrative fallacy is thus ubiquitous as a cascade of false assertions consistently snowballs into sweeping viral narratives.

Indeed, most political content on social media is plucked from an online-news ecosystem far different from traditional, pre-internet news media. Commentators that traditional gatekeepers would never have sanctioned are now hugely influential. As Thomas Patterson noted, "Breitbart News draws roughly 75 million monthly visitors. Even at its peak, the John Birch Society, the top alt-right outlet of its day, had fewer than 100,000 members." The resulting spread of misinformation is stunning: "One of the wilder ideas perpetrated by the Birchers was the claim that a 'one-world government' was being promoted by a shadowy group of conspirators, many of them holding powerful positions in Washington. Other than the Birchers, few Americans took the claim seriously. The notion got new life a few years ago when Breitbart," which has over two million Twitter followers, "began promoting it. Today, a third of Americans think it's true."

Third, social-media features such as Facebook's "Like" button and Twitter's "Retweet" button—both of which arose around 2010[70]—amplify controversial content that enflames tribal impulses. Incentives matter. And this new system incentivizes sensationalism over substance, accusation over evaluation, outrage over education. Journalists are now disproportionately focused on writing stories that will go viral on Facebook and Twitter, a very different goal from writing stories that will educate and inform. According to NYU professor Jonathan Haidt, "One of the engineers at Twitter who had worked on the 'Retweet' button later revealed that he regretted his contribution because it had made Twitter a nastier place. As he watched Twitter mobs forming through the use of the new tool, he thought to himself, 'We might have just handed a 4-year-old a loaded weapon.'" The new features also broadly trigger the availability bias as users are inundated with an avalanche of content (articles, videos, tweets, retweets, comments) surrounding one viral controversy after the other.

Fourth, social media degrades the political debate. It gets nasty. Users are often anonymous and therefore less concerned with social norms. They direct messages at strangers they'll never meet face to face. And bots are programmed to manipulate platforms and enflame divisiveness. This leads to frequent online harassment and consistently low-intelligence and anger-filled debate across the tribal divide.

Social media feeds are often cesspools of anger, idiocy, and resentment. Expressing views in America's new, twenty-first-century online public square can trigger an avalanche of hateful push-back. I have experienced this first hand. A

June 2023 column I wrote took the unremarkable position that America needs a competent president: "The President of the United States should be very competent. America has many such people. Millions even. And this basic litmus test shouldn't be controversial." Like many other commentators, on both the left and the right, I expressed concern about Joe Biden's age and declining mental capacities: "Now Biden, to be sure, has had a storied political career. His intentions are in the right place. And his administration is brimming with intelligent and highly competent public servants. But the man at the top—POTUS himself—is well past his prime."

The Twittersphere erupted. And Biden's tribe rushed to his defense. With mob fervor. Here are some highlights:

- "You're on the side that wants to keep racism alive and fresh."
- "What a joke."
- "No."
- "This is pure garbage."
- "You've got to be kidding with this insane and nauseating drivel."
- "A Jew's case for Hitler."
- "Incredibly lame."
- "Shame shame on you."
- "NO NO NO to the fuckity NO!!!"
- And my favorite: "This opinion eats doo-doo."

These folks had every right to express themselves. And as noted in Chapter 4, political speech—both high and low—should never be silenced. But as this social-media rot gains an ever greater foothold in America's public square, the body politic degenerates proportionately. "And what mainly fuels this," Andrew Sullivan explains, "is precisely what the Founders feared about democratic culture: feeling, emotion, and narcissism, rather than reason, empiricism, and public-spiritedness. Online debates become personal, emotional, and irresolvable almost as soon as they begin. Godwin's Law—it's only a matter of time before a comments section brings up Hitler—is a reflection of the collapse of the reasoned deliberation the Founders saw as indispensable to a functioning republic."

Finally, new technological innovations compound social media's harmful effects. Artificial intelligence, for example, promises to increase the potential of bots to manipulate platforms. And the ubiquity of fallacious narratives will only increase as deep fakes (sophisticated fake images and videos) appear to substantiate false stories.

Social media does some good, too. It connects people who would otherwise be strangers. It provides online communities to many who would otherwise be isolated from society. And, if used appropriately, it can be a valuable source of entertainment and education. Its negative effects, moreover, can be exaggerated. For example, contrary to some assertions, problems with self-esteem among teenagers existed long before Instagram's feed of happy pictures transformed the high-school experience.

But social media's capacity to increase bias and tribalism in America is highly consequential. Nothing has corresponded more closely with America's decline this century than the rise of social media.

(3) POLITICAL STRUCTURE

Because tribalism and social media exacerbate outrage and irrationality, a political and electoral structure that tames partisan passions is essential. America's does the opposite: it turbocharges them.

The biggest structural problem in American politics is the two-party system. As discussed in Chapter 5, ever since the mid-nineteenth century, two parties—the Democrats and the Republicans—have dominated America politics. Just as the founders feared. In his presidential farewell address, George Washington warned that, "The alternate domination of one faction over another, sharpened by the spirit of revenge, natural to party dissension, which in different ages and countries has perpetrated the most horrid enormities, is itself a frightful despotism." James Madison agreed, noting that "the public good is disregarded in the conflicts of rival parties." And John Adams was the most concerned of all: "a division of the republic into two great parties ... is to be dreaded as the greatest political evil."

With the separation of powers and federalism, the Constitution distributes *government* power far and wide. But it leaves *political* power unaddressed. The resulting two-party system has few restraints and channels America's volcanic political and electoral passions into two behemoth rival factions.

This extreme rivalry destabilizes the polity. If the Red Sox and Yankees played each other every single game, there'd be even more vitriol between the two baseball teams and their fans. Their competitive passions would be focused exclusively on each other. But Major League Baseball has twenty eight other teams, too. So while the Yanks and Sox have a strong rivalry, they forget about each other when they're playing other opponents.

The fewer tribes there are, the worse tribalism gets. And in America the two political tribes battle each other—and only each other—every single day. This myopic rivalry amplifies bias, distorts the political debate, warps the marketplace of ideas, shunts policy platforms, fuels outrage, and stifles compromise and negotiation. A deeply backward approach now dominates American politics: hating the other side even more than you like your own. A study published in *Science* magazine, titled *Political Sectarianism in America*,[71] highlighted this new paradigm: "Democrats and Republicans—the 85% of U.S. citizens who do not identify as pure independents—have grown more contemptuous of opposing partisans for decades, and at similar rates." Recently, the study continues, "this aversion exceeded their affection for copartisans."

These negative trends are accelerating. As social media has gained in prominence the two political parties have diverged further. Lee Drutman, the author of *Breaking the Two-Party Doom Loop: The Case for Multiparty Democracy in America*, explains that although "America's two-party system goes back centuries, the threat today is new and different because the two parties are now truly distinct, a development that I date to the 2010 midterms"—right when Twitter's "Retweet" and Facebook's "Like" features took hold. "Until then," Drutman continues, "the two parties contained enough overlapping multitudes within them that the sort of bargaining and coalition-building natural to multiparty democracy could work inside the two-party system. No

more. America now has just two parties, and that's it …
National politics transformed from a compromise-oriented
squabble over government spending into a zero-sum moral
conflict over national culture and identity. As the conflict
sharpened, the parties changed what they stood for. And as
the parties changed, the conflict sharpened further. Liberal
Republicans and conservative Democrats went extinct. The
four-party system collapsed into just two parties."

This political divergence has been swift and severe. As
Thomas Patterson explained in 2019, "the gap between
Republicans and Democrats on legalized abortion has
increased by a factor of five. On the question of human-caused
climate change, the gap is now nine times greater. In terms of
a ban on assault weapons, the divide has tripled." According to
Patterson, moreover, even by the "112th Congress (2011–12),
the middle had been hollowed out. As measured by roll-call
votes, the least conservative Republican in the House or Senate
was more conservative than the most conservative Democrat.
Four decades earlier, roughly a fourth of House and Senate
members were out of step with their party's majority—more
conservative in the case of Democrats and more liberal in the
case of Republicans."

A more diverse set of political parties would soften this
divide. It would invigorate mainstream political discourse
with additional points of view, as today many important
ideas don't make it onto the platforms of either side. The
introduction of new ideas and coalitions would reduce rigid
partisanship, help to calm bias and tribalism, and provide
incentives for politicians to respect empirical reality and not
just appease the incoherent batch of constituencies they hold

together with a shoestring (there is more on this phenomenon in the next chapter). As Drutman put it, a multi-party system would be "more fluid and responsive to Americans' political preferences" and help "dissolve our binary partisanship."

Additional political parties wouldn't solve everything, of course. The new parties' specific platforms would be of central importance. There would likely still be gridlock in Congress. Tribalism and social media wouldn't disappear. And other defects in the political system would remain. But a vibrant multi-party system would directly address and materially reduce the biggest problem in US politics: tribal rivalry and irrational partisanship that diverts people's attention from—and therefore undermines—the essential principles and traditions of American democracy.

A related structural deficiency is the closed-party primary election system. In closed primaries, which are common, only voters that register with a party may vote in that party's primary election.[72] In open primaries, by contrast, all voters, irrespective of party affiliation, can vote—thereby welcoming more moderates and independents into the fold. In his 2012 article, *The Electoral Origins of Polarized Politics: Evidence From the 2010 Cooperative Congressional Election Study*, Gary Jacobson explains, "Primary electoral constituencies tend to be even more extreme, particularly on the Republican side, deterring departures from party orthodoxy and thus movement toward the median voter." Jonathan Haidt thinks mandating open primaries would dramatically soften polarization: "If we simply eliminated closed party primaries and required all states and all elections to have open primaries, then elections would not be decided just by extremes. So that is one of the most important things, that is one of the big factors explaining why Congress became so polarized in the 1990s."

The two-party system exacerbates tribalism by pitting two large parties against each other without competition from other factions. Closed primaries deepen the divide. Meanwhile, several other structural problems undermine a central right of American citizens: the right to vote.

The first problem is gerrymandering. Every ten years the United States Census Bureau releases updated population and demographic data. States and local governments then perform redistricting—taking these data and drawing new voting-district boundaries. Because communities change over time, redistricting is an important democratic function. The maps must be redrawn so that districts are equally populated and comply with various laws. The goal is supposed to be straightforward: create maps that fairly and accurately reflect the population.

Gerrymandering turns this democratic objective into a political sham. Instead of drawing maps to equalize representation, controlling parties gerrymander by manipulating maps to dictate who gets elected. This deceitful practice has two main forms. *Cracking* occurs when legislators draw maps to split groups of people in the same political party across multiple districts. This dilutes those people's votes, reducing the likelihood they will elect their preferred candidate. *Packing* occurs when map-drawers cram groups of same-party voters into a small number of districts. This packs voters into select districts, helping them there but weakening the same party's vote in other districts.

While the process takes place in the open, the consequences are sinister. If one person is disenfranchised, that is one too many. By artificially placing voters in districts where the outcome is effectively predetermined, America's large-scale gerrymandering disenfranchises millions. A 2019 report by the Center for American Progress[73] found that gerrymandering "shifted, on average, a whopping 59 seats in the U.S. House of Representatives during the 2012, 2014, and 2016 elections. That means that every other November, 59 politicians that would not have been elected based on statewide voter support for their party won anyway because the lines were drawn in their favor—often by their allies in the Republican or Democratic Party." A change of 59 seats, the report explained, "is slightly more than the total number of seats apportioned to the 22 smallest states by population. It is also more than the number of representatives for America's largest state, California, which has 53 House members representing a population of nearly 40 million people."

The extent of this scourge shouldn't be surprising. Gerrymandering stems from one of the main reasons America isn't working: a population of biased tribal warriors hooked on social media will eventually, inevitably, produce like-minded government officials. While there may be a lag, the more biased and tribal the populace, the more biased and tribal the government will be. As Franklin Delano Roosevelt explained, the American government and the American people are one and the same: "Let us never forget that government is ourselves and not an alien power over us. The ultimate rulers of our democracy are not a President and

Senators and Congressmen and government officials, but the voters of this country."

Gerrymandering is a quintessential example of how Americans cast aside their own Constitutional principles and essential traditions in a zero-sum, two-party battle for political dominance. The Electoral College also broadly dilutes the vote. Unlike gerrymandering, however, the Electoral College is a legitimate Constitutional system. It's nonetheless outdated, overly complicated, and deeply counterproductive.

The Electoral College is a group of intermediaries that helps select the president. The founders' aim with the Electoral College was to tame the populace's passions by limiting their control over presidential elections. Each state is allocated presidential electors in proportion to its federal representatives and senators. As we saw in Chapter 3, this gave the Electoral College a dark history as the Constitution's Three-Fifths Clause increased the number of electors for slave-holding states. Today, the Electoral College has 538 electors, and presidential candidates must gain at least 270 to win.

State legislatures decide how to appoint their electors. As the general election approaches, political parties within states typically nominate slates of would-be electors. The in-state election outcome determines which party's slate (the Democrats' or the Republicans') will be made into actual electors. Then the national Electoral College convenes. And on January 6, Congress counts the electoral votes and declares the winner. (As we'll see in Chapter 9, part of Donald

Trump's plan to overthrow the 2020 presidential election involved thwarting this process.)

The first big problem with the Electoral College is that by tying electors to Congressional representation, smaller states (with the same number of senators as larger ones) have outsized influence. As Harvard University political scientist Gautam Mukunda put it, "The fact that in presidential elections people in Wyoming have [nearly four] times the power of people in California is antithetical at the most basic level to what we say we stand for as a democracy."

The second big problem is that the Electoral College forces campaigns to focus on only a few "swing states" such as (in recent years) Wisconsin, Michigan, and Nevada. Many other states, such as New York, New Hampshire, and Arkansas, are foregone conclusions and get ignored. Here's the rub: the presidential election is really just a concentrated competition in a handful of states, none of which represent the country as a whole. Five presidents have been elected, including two of the last six (both Republicans) without winning the national popular vote. "In no other country in the world that considers itself a democracy can the loser of the popular vote be deemed the winner of the election," Berkeley Law Dean Erwin Chemerinsky noted. "The Electoral College is inconsistent with the most basic notions of democracy."

Of course, this might change if Republicans focused more on large states that they now (rationally) ignore. So the common argument that the Electoral College favors Republicans is overstated. But today this bizarre system creates a striking absurdity: most Americans cast meaningless votes in presidential elections. And they know it. Jesse

Wegman, the author of *Let the People Pick the President: The Case for Abolishing the Electoral College*, explains: "If anything, representative democracy in the 21st century is about political equality. It's about one person, one vote—everybody's vote counting equally. You're not going to convince a majority of Americans that that's not how you should do it." Pew Research reported in September 2023, moreover, that "nearly two-thirds of U.S. adults (65%) say the way the president is elected should be changed so that the winner of the popular vote nationwide wins the presidency."

These concerns about the franchise are compounded by the Supreme Court's current composition. The president can only appoint justices when there's a vacancy, usually as a result of the death of a justice or a justice's voluntary decision to step down. The number of appointments per president is therefore arbitrary (in four-year terms, Jimmy Carter got none and Donald Trump got three). In a country where 55 percent of the people voted for a Democratic president, Republican presidents have appointed six of the nine justices.

This result is constitutionally permissible and it's legitimate for the court to be counter-majoritarian. But—on top of everything else—it compounds Americans' frustration with their government. A "rogue" Supreme Court, many think, has pitted the Constitution against the public. After the court overruled *Roe v. Wade* along partisan lines, *New York Times* columnist Jamelle Bouie wrote that a "reckless, reactionary and power-hungry" Supreme Court shouldn't "exist above the constitutional system." The *Economist* piled on, asserting that a "less exceptional" America has "a set of federal laws that do not reflect what Americans actually want." And even liberal justice Elena Kagan warned that if "the court loses all connection with the public and the public sentiment, that's a dangerous thing for democracy." Setting aside whether these sentiments are accurate, they reflect growing indignation among America's political majority that their views don't matter.

In sum, the two-party system creates a bitter rivalry between two mega-tribes; closed primaries sharpen the divide; gerrymandering disenfranchises millions of Americans; the Electoral College renders the votes of tens of millions more irrelevant; and the highest court in the land consistently defines the Constitution in strident opposition to the people's majority preferences. When the resulting anger and frustration are combined with already enflamed tribal biases and then run through the social-media outrage machine, the result is as predictable as it is alarming: a polity on fire.

7

Political Dysfunction

*"It is useless to attempt to reason a man out of a
thing he was never reasoned into"*
Jonathan Swift

This combination of America's tribalism, social media, and
political structure whips up a pulsating frenzy of political
dysfunction. The frenzy has several related and overlapping
elements.

INCOHERENCE
First, there's little intellectual coherence with respect to
political parties or affiliations, other than one's strict allegiance
to his or her tribe. Being a Democrat or Republican, or a
liberal or conservative, has less to do with any consistent
philosophical underpinning and more to do with loyally
supporting your team and, even more importantly, opposing
the other side. Sure, Democrats tend to favor bigger
government and more inclusive politics. And Republicans
tend to favor freer markets and less government intervention,

in theory at least. But in the day-to-day grind of American politics, these and other supposed principles tend to disappear.

The result is that neither tribe has a principled set of beliefs. For example, there's no necessary intellectual connection whatsoever between being in favor of (1) strict laws limiting abortion, (2) lower taxes, and (3) higher military spending. Yet these are three central tenets of the modern-day Republican platform—today at least—and tens of millions of Republicans therefore believe in all of them, deep in their bones.

Likewise, there's no reason why any single person should necessarily favor (1) an expansive social safety net, (2) lower military spending, and (3) robust regulations to protect the environment. Yet, again, these are central tenets of the Democratic platform—for now—and tens of millions of Democrats therefore passionately believe in all of them.

These arbitrary platforms stem from party leadership strategically cobbling together disparate blocs of voters. But the aim of a party's leadership isn't intellectual coherence; it's to build coalitions, to get more votes, to win elections. Republicans accordingly cater to wealthy individuals (who want lower taxes), weapons manufacturers (who want more military spending), and evangelicals (who want pro-life judges); and Democrats cater to the social-security lobby (who want to protect the safety net), progressives (who want to spend less on defense and more on social programs), and environmentalists (who want to subsidize clean energy).

There's no reason for most Americans to fall in line with either of these disjointed platforms. They should think things through for themselves and have a consistent, principled, personal set of beliefs. Instead, they simply turn to their tribe. As Oliver Burkeman explained, "Tell Republicans that some imaginary policy is a Republican one, as the psychologist Geoffrey Cohen did in 2003,[74] and they're much more likely to support it, even if it runs counter to Republican values. But ask them why they support it, and they'll deny that party affiliation played a role. Cohen found something similar for Democrats."

Richard Nixon's "Southern Strategy" exemplifies how party leaders strategically attract blocs of disparate voters. Many southern Democrats were angry after their party, led by President Lyndon Johnson, passed the Civil Rights Act of 1964, which outlawed racial segregation.[75] Nixon and the Republicans pounced on the opportunity. Using thinly veiled racist rhetoric, they appealed to these southern voters. As author Ferrel Guillory explains, "[I]n his 1968 campaign and afterward, Nixon used coded language, political symbolism and court interventions as signals to southern white voters." It worked. Nixon won two presidential elections with a larger Republican party behind him. And the Republicans, in turn, used their electoral wins to pass laws (like pro-business legislation) that mattered little to these former southern Democrats.

INCONSISTENCY
This incoherence breeds inconsistency. American politics is throbbing with tribal-driven flip-flops and contradictory zigzags. Lacking sturdy intellectual underpinnings, both sides lurch from one position to a contradictory one with stunning regularity. A few illustrations (plucked from an ocean of examples) establish the point.

Let's start with the Democrats. They demonized Presidents George W. Bush and Donald Trump for attacking the press; yet they gave President Obama a pass while his Department of Justice set records for prosecuting reporters. They accused Bush of illicitly expanding executive power during his "war on terror." Yet they looked the other way when Obama aggressively expanded executive power to address immigration. They said Trump turned the presidency into a fascist dictatorship (quite an accomplishment if true), while also maintaining that Trump was too stupid to get anything done. They said major social-justice protests during the Covid-19 pandemic were necessary and important, but that Republican political rallies were reckless. They said gay marriage is a fundamental, non-negotiable right. Then they negotiated with themselves and gave Biden a pass in 2020 for voting against legalizing gay marriage in 1996. They said men's inappropriate interactions with women can never be tolerated. Then they tolerated Biden's inappropriate interactions with women when they became public during the presidential campaign.

The list goes on. And on. And on.

Republicans are even worse. They fiercely opposed the individual mandate in Obama's 2010 health-care plan. But this was a conservative innovation championed by Republican Governor (and 2012 GOP presidential nominee) Mitt Romney. They stood proud as the self-proclaimed party of unwavering virtue and decency, especially after Bill Clinton's impeachment as a result of his affair with a White House intern. But Donald Trump—the least virtuous and least decent president in American history—became their champion. They were fiercely anti-Russian, Cold-War warriors when Obama was president (Romney in 2012: "Russia is, without question, our number one geopolitical foe"), but when Trump came along saying nice things about Vladimir Putin, Russia wasn't so bad after all. They were staunchly pro-free trade for decades, including when Obama was president. Then when Trump aggressively used tariffs they switched sides.

And on. And on. And on.

Lots of political inconsistency goes both ways. The opposition party in Congress often threatens government shutdowns to get their way. And the party in power is always aghast that their opponents would stoop so low. When your guy is in office, Congress should only impeach a president for the most serious offenses. When the other guy is the accused, however, the standard plummets into a highly elastic "political question" reserved for Congress's whims. When lunatics from your side commit violent crimes in the name of politics, they are isolated whackos. If they are politically on the other side, though, there's a direct causal link: the violence was an inevitable consequence of the opposing party's nefarious platform and irresponsible leadership.

Some inconsistency is myopically results-driven. The flip-flop of Republican senators from Merrick Garland (no election-year Supreme Court confirmations) to Amy Coney Barrett (ram the nomination through weeks before the election) got them an extra justice. Some of it is rank partisanship. Democrats turn a blind eye to Joe Biden's obvious declining capacities after spending four years claiming Donald Trump's incompetence threatened the republic. And some inconsistency goes fundamentally against the supposed core ideology of the party itself. The dramatic increase in federal spending under Trump and the Republicans was jaw-dropping—even by today's low standards—after Republicans spent eight years righteously opposing Obama's budgets in the name of Republican-style fiscal discipline.

The common thread tying together this tangled web of contradiction is a feverish and exclusive focus on short-term political objectives. Cast aside in the tumult is not just any pretense of consistency, but respect for and adherence to the Constitutional principles and essential traditions that have made America work since its founding.

DELUSIONS

Twenty-first-century American politics isn't just incoherent and inconsistent. It's often downright delusional. Americans consistently accept or reject versions of reality based simply on their politics. Again, these aren't merely quirks at the margins. Americans have very extreme and highly divergent views about the empirical world's basic contours.

Millions of conservatives, for instance, have long believed that Hillary Clinton and other Democrats ran a child sex ring out of Washington DC's Comet Ping Pong pizza shop. And millions of liberals have long believed that George W. Bush purposefully allowed the September 11, 2001 terrorist attacks to help him geopolitically. Thomas Patterson highlights examples of widespread falsehoods (and the percentage of Americans who believe them) in his 2019 book *How America*

Lost Its Mind: The Assault on Reason That's Crippling Our Democracy:

- "Donald Trump won the popular vote in the 2016 election (20 percent)."
- "Iraqis used weapons of mass destruction against U.S. troops during the Iraq invasion (20 percent)."
- "The 2010 Affordable Care Act includes 'death panels' (40 percent)."
- "Childhood vaccines cause autism (15 percent)."
- "Global warming is a hoax (35 percent)."
- "Russia didn't meddle in the 2016 presidential election (37 percent)."

These beliefs aren't just delusional. They're dangerous. They seep into the bloodstream of American politics, proliferate on social media, and render large swaths of the electorate—from both political tribes—wholly detached from reality.

LIES

There are inconsistencies, there are delusions, and then there are lies. And lies have come to permeate American politics. The King of Lies is, of course, none other than the 45th president of the United States. As Professor Robert Prentice explains: "President Donald Trump's lying is 'off the charts.' No prominent politician in memory bests Trump for spouting spectacular, egregious, easily disproved lies The birther claim. The vote fraud claim. The attendance at the inauguration claim. And on and on and on. Every fact checker—Kessler, Factcheck.org, Snopes.com, PolitiFact—finds a level of mendacity unequaled by any politician ever scrutinized. For instance, 70 percent of his campaign statements checked by PolitiFact were mostly false, totally false, or 'pants on fire' false."

Here's a small sampling of Donald Trump's lies to the American people while he was president:

- "Just stay calm. It will go away." (About Covid 19 on March 10, 2020.)
- "The overall audience was, I think, the biggest ever to watch an inauguration address, which was a great thing."
- "Terrible! Just found out that Obama had my 'wires tapped' in Trump Tower just before the victory. Nothing found. This is McCarthyism!"
- "The NSA and FBI tell Congress that Russia did not influence electoral process."
- "We got 306 because people came out and voted like they've never seen before so that's the way it goes. I guess it was the biggest Electoral College win since Ronald Reagan."
- "It is a disgrace that my full Cabinet is still not in place, the longest such delay in the history of our country. Obstruction by Democrats!"
- "And yet the murder rate in our country is the highest it's been in 47 years, right? Did you know that? Forty-seven years."
- "I've gotten tremendous business to go to Michigan. Michigan is one of the reasons I ran. I was honored in

Michigan long before I thought about—I was honored as the Man of the Year in Michigan at a big event."

Trump's lying is so pathological that he often lies about other people lying. "Look at all the lies he's told," Trump said, with a straight face, about Joe Biden in September 2023. "Everything he says is like a lie. It's terrible!"

Politicians are rarely paragons of truth and probity. No doubt. But before Trump, neither were they shameless propagandists spewing endless lies—lies that everyone knows are lies—from the nation's highest office. The erosion of America's political norms cannot be overstated. Trump's dishonesty is a license for other politicians to lie themselves: *if the president is a pathological liar, then I can lie, too.* It also makes typical political improprieties seem trivial by comparison: *if the president is lying every day to the American people, who cares if I'm a little shady in my home district.* A whole generation of young Americans are coming of age politically as the polity swirls in a torrent of lies.

IGNORANCE

Yet another dysfunction compounding the delirium is Americans' ignorance of their representative democracy's basic elements. Americans focus little on human history, let alone absorb its lessons. And an embarrassing percentage of them don't understand basic civics.

The Annenberg Public Policy Center at the University of Pennsylvania has conducted the Civics Knowledge Survey since 2006.[76] The 2022 findings include the following jaw-droppers:

- "Less than half (47%) of U.S. adults could name all three branches of government (executive, legislative, judicial) ... One in 4 respondents could not name any."
- "Over half of Americans (51%) continue to assert incorrectly that Facebook is required to let all Americans express themselves freely on its platform under the First Amendment."
- "1 in 5 (22%) incorrectly thinks that it is accurate to say that under the Constitution a president can ignore a Supreme Court ruling if the president believes it is wrong."
- "Nearly 1 in 3 people (32%) incorrectly thinks that a judge has the prerogative to force a defendant to testify at trial."
- "Asked what it means when the Supreme Court rules 5–4 in a case, just over half (55%) correctly chose 'the decision is the law and needs to be followed.'"
- "When asked unprompted to name the protections specified in the First Amendment:[77]
    o One in 4 respondents (26%) said they can't name any or don't know
    o Freedom of speech was cited by 63%
    o Freedom of religion was named by 24%
    o Freedom of the press was named by 20%
    o Right of assembly was named by 16%
    o Right to petition the government was named by 6%"

Yikes.

Eleanor Roosevelt (1884–1962) set forth the basic standard for civic education in America: "Our children should learn the general framework of their government and then they should know where they come in contact with the government, where it touches their daily lives and where their influence is exerted on the government. It must not be a distant thing, someone else's business, but they must see how every cog in the wheel of a democracy is important and bears its share of responsibility for the smooth running of the entire machine."

The former first lady would shudder at today's ignorance and apathy. And she'd agree that a main reason why America isn't working is because far too many Americans don't know how it's supposed to work.

One reason why so many Americans shun civics is simple: because they can. The nation's long-sustained material prosperity and geopolitical tranquility allow them to focus on other things, like sports, celebrity scandal, and their own personal circumstances. To the extent they consider it at all, many Americans take for granted that the political system will function effectively. They shouldn't. History has never been kind to political apathy and ignorance.

HARD QUESTIONS
All of this dysfunction renders America virtually incapable of wrestling with sensitive and hard public-policy questions, which sit idle and unaddressed in a haze of anger, delusion, and irrationality. As the *New York Times*' David Brooks puts it, there's been "a breakdown in America's ability to face evidence objectively, to pay due respect to reality, to deal with complex and unpleasant truths. Once a country tolerates dishonesty, incuriosity and intellectual laziness, then everything else falls apart."

Not every public-policy question is complicated or hard to sort out. Some are easy: More of the ultra-rich's wealth should be redistributed to the poor. A strong and smart military is essential. The education system should be strengthened in underserved communities. Election integrity is paramount.

But some policy questions are hard. They involve competing considerations and difficult line-drawing. And they require nuance, compromise, and subtlety to work through.

Take abortion. One tribe screams: it's a woman's right to choose! The other howls: protect unborn children! Both sides seldom acknowledge that the other has a valid concern. Yet both do. Women should have the fundamental right to determine their own reproductive choices—not have this imposed upon them by the government. And under no circumstances—ever—should a woman's life be put at risk by carrying a fetus. If men had not unfairly dominated government for most of history, there would be little precedent for state intrusions into this sphere of women's liberty.

At the same time, however, wanting to protect an unborn fetus is a valid impulse. Setting aside when a fetus becomes a life—a question without a clear answer—we can all agree that a healthy fetus will most likely *become* a life. This truth should be given at least *some* weight by everyone, especially the further into pregnancy abortion is allowed. Avoidable, late-term abortions should give everyone pause. And the government does (and is supposed to) consistently intervene to protect vulnerable potential victims of harm.

How does one harmonize these competing concerns? The answer is as unsatisfying as it is unavoidable: they can't be.

Sometimes a policy question has no options that don't include bad outcomes. It's both zero-sum and debated across a continuum with no truly satisfactory solutions. That is, sometimes no matter where on the policy continuum the line is drawn, some people will be negatively or unfairly impacted—and fully optimizing the competing interests is still riddled with problems. This should be openly acknowledged by all sides. And extreme, categorical positions should be recognized for what they are: too simple.

Another example of a hard policy question involves transgender teenagers and sports. A teenage boy who decides to become a girl should be respected, supported, and celebrated. The underlying circumstance will have been challenging and the decision to transition courageous. And that child's classmates, school, and community play an essential role in protecting and supporting that child.

Yet, at the same time, when the transition leads to significant unfair advantages in sports, a competing consideration emerges: the integrity of sport for all participants. This is essential in its own right. Sports play a fundamental role in American society and in the lives of kids who grow up playing them. For other girls to be dominated physically by transgender athletes due to biological differences isn't fair.

How does one harmonize *these* competing concerns? Again, the answer is both unsatisfactory and obvious: they can't be. Communities just have to muddle through the best they can. Polarized assertions over-simplifying things— from one extreme or the other—are as counterproductive as they are stupid.

A third example of a really complex and controversial policy topic is the correct role for police in American society. The debate here is often radically over-simplified. "Black lives matter!" (Yes, of course.) "Blue lives matter!" (True, too.) "Defund the police!" (Say, what?) "Refund the police!" (Train them too, please.)

On the one hand, police brutality is real. Police officers do commit crimes against those they are supposed to protect. Some subset of police officers are, in fact, racist. And America's history with racism magnifies the harms and sensitivities surrounding this abuse. On the other hand, the police are absolutely necessary for reducing crime. Most police officers aren't racist. And a strong police force protects innocent, vulnerable, law-abiding citizens, including those in underprivileged communities.

All of this is true at the same time.

George Floyd's murder by a Minneapolis police officer was every bit as horrific as the most impassioned social-justice warriors assert. Yet the extent to which Americans—online, in the press, and in the streets—called for defunding the police and interpreted *all* use of force by the police as criminal was counterproductive. And deeply so. It predictably caused the police to withdraw from inner cities, contributing to increased violence there.[78, 79] Sometimes cause and effect are hard to tease out with public policy. This one's easy: the more police officers are unfairly accused of criminal violence, the less likely they are to proactively stop crime.

How should one wrestle with the competing considerations *here*? For starters, one must recognize that a perfect line can't be drawn on the policy continuum: a police force large and proactive enough to sufficiently deter crime will inevitably commit some amount of gratuitous violence. Bad apples must be limited, but they will never be eliminated. Pretending otherwise helps no one. The key is to strike the right balance: police forces should be sufficiently staffed and insulated legally to meet the specific needs of their communities; and they should also be adequately trained and regulated to minimize misconduct. Extreme views have no place in this calculus.

America's failure to grapple with hard questions has consequences. Big consequences. Take America's biggest failure to do so this century: its response to the Covid-19 pandemic. Here Americans' tribalism, social-media addiction, and Democrat-versus-Republican super-rivalry all culminated in a large-scale policy catastrophe.

The pandemic raised really hard policy questions, to be sure. Simple solutions were elusive. There was plenty of room for legitimate disagreement. And things are much clearer now, in hindsight. But neither side struck a rational balance with its approach. Many on the left didn't weigh heavily enough (or at all) the profound economic and psychological impact of shutting down businesses and schools by government fiat. Nor did they remember that governmental authority is vested in elected officials and not the experts who advise them. And they made far too many credibility-straining overstatements about Covid's impact—which was largely confined to people with serious health problems and the elderly.

But conservatives were a whole lot worse. Tens of millions of them refused to take even simple measures to protect themselves and others from a pandemic that would end up killing millions. Instead of simply wearing masks, avoiding large indoor gatherings, and getting vaccinated, they railed against these prudent policies just as hard as they did against the imprudent policies. The consequence wasn't just being wrong. Lots of people died who otherwise wouldn't have.

As is now typical, there was no logic or necessary reason for the political divide to be drawn as it was. Conservatives could just as easily have been pro-vaccine, giving the incumbent Republican administration credit (rightly or wrongly) for the vaccines' speedy development. And liberals could just as easily have rallied around keeping schools open, as lower-income students were among the worst hit by school closures. For whatever arbitrary reasons, the ideological lines were etched as they were. And once they gained traction, the tribal bandwagons piled on.

The optimal response to Covid 19 would have been measured, balancing protecting vulnerable populations with tailored health measures against the heavy toll of closing schools and businesses. Few advocated for this approach. Americans' reflex of running to extremes and addressing complicated policy challenges with the blunt weaponry of tribal warfare—reinforced by years of muscle memory—was simply too strong to shake off.

The government response to Covid 19 exemplifies how low the American polity has sunk in the twenty-first century. At the start of the century, Americans banded together when confronted with a national challenge: the terrorist attacks on September 11, 2001. Andrew Kohut of Pew Research, for example, analyzed a number of public-opinion surveys in March 2002 and concluded that "the attacks not only generated a burst of national unity and patriotism, but also increased the public's trust in government and in the relevance of political leaders." This made sense: terrorism threatened every American in one way or another. Twenty years later when confronted with another national challenge, Americans immediately fractured along the same polarized two-party divide that governs trivial day-to-day political squabbles. A similar overriding logic was present: Covid 19 threatened every American in one way or another. But the response was radically dissimilar to the response to the terrorist attacks in 2001. The American body politic had fundamentally changed in the intervening twenty years.

Twenty-first-century America had become a very different place.

8

Policy Failures

> *"We don't really worry about climate change because it's too overwhelming and we're already in too deep. It's like if you owe your bookie $1,000, you're like, 'OK, I've got to pay this dude back.' But if you owe your bookie $1 million, you're like, 'I guess I'm just going to die.'"*
> Colin Jost, *Saturday Night Live*

The response to Covid 19 exemplifies how dysfunctional America has become as social media exacerbates tribalism within the two-party political system. That travesty, however, was hardly America's only twenty-first-century public-policy failure. There are many. As America's elected officials are consumed by myopic, negative-sum political disputes, their constituents' desperate needs consistently go unaddressed.

As we learned in Chapter 1, human history shows that governing is hard. Doing everything well in a country of 335 million people is impossible. And America does get a lot of things right, even now. The world's oldest constitutional democracy is nonetheless dramatically underperforming in the policy arena. The trends are broad and powerful, and they're accelerating in the wrong direction.

INEQUALITY

First, as noted in Chapter 5, the distribution of wealth in America is grotesquely uneven. One can find, in the same American city—indeed on the same American street—individuals worth billions of dollars (more than the GDP of numerous countries)[80] and people without a home or reliable source of food. In a country with tens of thousands of millionaires, on a single representative night in 2022, 582,000 Americans were homeless.[81]

This is as addressable as it is insane: merely redistributing one percent of the richest Americans' wealth—many billions of dollars—could alleviate tremendous human suffering. And it keeps getting worse. According to *Forbes* magazine, "In 1987, the [world's] 140 billionaires had an aggregate net worth of $295 billion." By 2021, "2,755 billionaires [were] worth $13.1 trillion." *Forbes* continued: "The United States still boasts the most billionaires, with 735 ... worth a collective $4.5 trillion." And America's corporate titans rule: "Amazon's Jeff Bezos is the world's richest for the fourth year running, worth $177 billion, while Tesla's Elon Musk ranked second with $151 billion. The top 10 richest" from around the world "are worth $1.15 trillion."

To put this in perspective, according to Oxfam International in January 2023, $1.7 trillion a year is "enough to lift *two billion people* out of poverty."[82] (Author's emphasis.)

The problem isn't just the ultra-rich, though. As Pew Research notes, America's upper class is getting richer as its middle class shrinks: "The growth in income in recent decades has tilted to upper-income households. At the same time, the U.S. middle class, which once comprised the clear majority of Americans, is shrinking. Thus, a greater share of the nation's aggregate income is now going to upper-income households and the share going to middle- and lower-income households is falling. The share of American adults who live in middle-income households has decreased from 61% in 1971 to 51% in 2019."

Moreover, America's inequality is worse than other wealthy nations. The Gini coefficient is a common measure of a country's inequality. It measures inequality from 0 (perfect equality) to 1 (complete inequality). According to the Organization for Economic Co-operation and Development in 2017, "the Gini coefficient in the U.S. stood at 0.434." This number "was higher than in any other of the G-7 countries, in which the Gini ranged from 0.326 in France to 0.392 in the UK, and inching closer to the level of inequality observed in India (0.495)."

There are many drivers of this inequality. To name a few: technological automation; inherited wealth; insufficient corporate regulation; liberal trade policies; outsourced labor; a deficient tax system; and a broken public-education system. Some inequality, however, is driven by individual choice (people opting to spend time on less-profitable activities) and work ethic (some people just work harder than others). And there's nothing necessarily wrong with getting rich. A relatively large amount of inequality should even be encouraged. Hard work and ingenuity should be rewarded, as wealth first needs to be created before it can be redistributed.

And big success stories motivate others to innovate and take risks that improve society at large. Innovation would plummet if entrepreneurs had severe caps on their income.

But an excessive, gratuitous, *pathological* level of inequality poisons society. The same nation shouldn't have a few jackpot winners worth hundreds of billions of dollars and tens of millions struggling to get by.

"Twenty-first-century America," economist Nicholas Eberstadt observed, "has somehow managed to produce markedly more wealth for its wealthholders even as it provided markedly less work for its workers."

This jarring asymmetry causes widespread resentment. It reduces trust in government. It erodes national unity and cohesion. And it fuels bias and tribalism, creating fertile ground for populism and demagoguery.

America-led globalization created the international marketplace that allowed companies like Apple, Amazon, and Google to become trillion-dollar behemoths, and their largest shareholders to reap unfathomable bounties. But it also caused millions of Americans to lose their jobs.[83] Traditionally American-made products, like steel and electronics, are now produced overseas, in China and elsewhere, and imported at cheap prices. While this new system lowered prices for consumers generally, it also shattered vulnerable American families, bankrupted successful small businesses, and hollowed out proud communities. We'll revisit this point in Chapter 9, but these losses generate bitter anger toward government elites—the architects of globalization—especially on the right within the white working class. Author and now US Senator from Ohio J. D .Vance explains the phenomenon in his 2016 book *Hillbilly Elegy*: "There is a cultural movement in the white working class to blame problems on society or the government, and that movement gains adherents by the day." Vance continued: "What separates the successful from the unsuccessful are the expectations that they had for their own lives. Yet the message of the right is increasingly: it's not your fault that you're a loser; it's the government's fault."

This is the fertile soil from which Donald Trump rose. The wily opportunist (and billionaire) from New York fanned these flames during his 2016 presidential campaign. "We can't continue to allow China to rape our country, and that's what they're doing," Trump said to cheering fans on the trail. "We have a lot to overcome in our country," he said at another campaign rally, "especially the fact that our jobs are being taken away from us and going to other places ... In this new future," with Trump at the helm, "millions of workers on the sidelines will return to the workforce."

Trump's 2016 electoral strategy of enflaming bitterness about America's role in the global economic system was stunningly successful. He won by promising to change things back to the way they were before, to "make America great again." Yet today, globalization marches on. The ultra-rich are richer still. The struggles of the poor and disrupted remain immense—as does their corresponding populist resentment. And the distribution of wealth in American society grows ever more uneven.

CRIMINAL JUSTICE
America's criminal-justice system reinforces socio-economic inequality, pumping still more tribal anger into the system.

In his 1903 book *The Souls of Black Folk*, W. E. B. Du Bois wrote that, "Daily the Negro is coming more and more to look upon law and justice, not as protecting safeguards, but as sources of humiliation and oppression. The laws are made by men who have little interest in him; they are executed by men who have absolutely no motive for treating the black people with courtesy or consideration; and, finally, the accused law-breaker is tried, not by his peers, but too often by men who would rather punish ten innocent Negroes than let one guilty one escape."

Many think little has changed.

A huge number of Americans—disproportionately those from underprivileged backgrounds—are trapped in a cruel and senseless system of mass incarceration. According to New York University's Brennan Center for Justice, "The United States has less than five percent of the world's population and nearly one-quarter of its prisoners. Astonishingly, if the 2.3 million incarcerated Americans were a state, it would be more populous than 16 other states. All told, one in three people in the United States has some type of criminal record. No other industrialized country comes close."

But America doesn't just imprison too many people. While incarcerated, people are often subject to unconscionable abuse and neglect. Long-time political prisoner and former President of South Africa Nelson Mandela once said, "[N]o one truly knows a nation until one has been inside its jails. A nation should not be judged by how it treats its highest citizens, but its lowest ones." Yes, indeed. And America's performance under Mandela's standard is shameful. Its jails are consistently overcrowded, under-resourced, and without proper oversight. The United States Justice Department, for example, detailed conditions in Alabama's state-run prisons in 2018. "The violations are severe, systemic, and exacerbated by serious deficiencies in staffing and supervision," the DOJ explained. There was "a high level of violence that is too common, cruel, of an unusual nature, and pervasive."

The costs of this system, moreover, are immense. As the Brennan Center explained, "Mass incarceration has crushing consequences: racial, social, and economic. We spend around $270 billion per year on our criminal justice system. In California it costs more than $75,000 per year to house each prisoner—more than it would cost to send them to Harvard." And the socio-economic impact is incalculable: "Mass incarceration exacerbates poverty and inequality, serving as an economic ball and chain that holds back millions, making it harder to find a job, access public benefits, and reintegrate into the community." According to the *New York Times*, "An estimated 60 percent of those leaving prison are unemployed a year later." Worse still, many with criminal records can't vote. This distorts the franchise—preventing truly free and fair elections—and undermines reform initiatives in Washington and state capitals. A constituency that can't vote has a long, hard road to achieving meaningful reform.

Mass incarceration has several underlying causes. Mandatory minimum sentences require judges to sentence defendants convicted of certain crimes to minimum—and often excessive—sentences. Michelle Alexander describes the resulting injustice: "All of us violate the law at some point in our lives. In fact, if the worst thing you have ever done is speed ten miles over the speed limit on the freeway, you have put yourself and others at more risk of harm than someone smoking marijuana in the privacy of his or her living room. Yet there are people in the United States serving life sentences for first-time drug offenses, something virtually unheard of anywhere else in the world."

Legal representation for underprivileged defendants, moreover, is abysmal. Poor defendants are typically saddled with overburdened or incompetent attorneys. According to attorney Bryan Stevenson, "Our criminal justice system treats you better if you are rich and guilty than if you are poor and innocent." And the court system is often arbitrary and capricious. Judges are overworked. Prosecutors enjoy large budgets, broad discretion to pursue charges, and immunity for bad acts. And juries—the system's linchpin—are prone to bias, prejudice, and delivering erroneous verdicts.

Put simply, the whole system is stacked against underprivileged defendants from start to finish.

While the full scope of these deficiencies are appreciated by few Americans who aren't directly affected by them, some awareness, at least, of the injustice is emerging. But it's still far too little. According to Gallup in 2023, "The latest poll also finds Americans are evenly divided in their views of whether people accused of committing crimes are treated fairly by the criminal justice system. Equal 49% shares of U.S. adults say such suspects are treated very or somewhat fairly and very or somewhat unfairly. This marks a significant shift in opinion compared with prior readings in 2000 and 2003, when two-thirds of Americans said criminal suspects were treated at least somewhat fairly."

A functioning society does, of course, need a criminal-justice system. Enforcing laws fairly and proportionately deters criminal behavior and provides important redress to victims. And many guilty people do deserve to be punished. But the degree of over-incarceration in America—and the corresponding societal harm—is a staggering failure of both governance and conscience.

EDUCATION

Yet another failure reinforcing inequality and injustice is America's public-education system, which educates over 90 percent of America's K–12 students.[84] A nation's public schools reflect both its current consciousness and its future prospects. America's founders recognized this. John Adams insisted that the education of "every rank and class of people, down to the lowest and the poorest" always had "to be the care of the public" and "maintained at the public expense." And "no expense ... would be too extravagant." Adams, moreover, wrote the 1780 Massachusetts Constitution, which declared that "wisdom and knowledge ... diffused generally among the body of the people [are] necessary for the preservation of their rights and liberties ... [Thus,] it shall be the duty of legislatures and magistrates, in all future periods of this commonwealth, to cherish the ... public schools." And Thomas Jefferson, for his part, aimed to build a robust public-education system in his home state of Virginia. He understood that an educated populace was a crucial defense against demagoguery. In his "Bill for the More General Diffusion of Knowledge," Jefferson warned that government "tyranny" would emerge unless "the people at large" were "educated at the common expense of all."

Recognizing the importance of public education was hardly the founders' greatest insight. Its importance is perfectly obvious. A nation's well-being will always correspond, over time, to the quality of its schools. As Cicero noted centuries ago, "What society does to its children, so will its children do to society." Yet while America's public-education system has historically been a success, it is deteriorating in the twenty-first century. This is a monumental unforced error.

The problems are manifold.[85] Low and declining rates of government funding are leading to less talent and commitment among teachers, who are severely underpaid. Teachers' unions often make this worse by protecting under-performers. Budget deficits cause overcrowded classrooms and limit essential resources like new books and in-classroom technology. And rivalries with charter schools and voucher programs divert funds away from public schools.

A decline in school safety, moreover, is having a negative psychological impact on students. High-profile shootings on campuses shake the nation. Bullying is also a big problem. According to the National Center for Education Statistics in 2018, over 20 percent of students in grades 6 through 12 have been bullied either in school or on their way to/from school.[86] Studies show increased mental-health challenges among students, especially in college.

These struggles get worse the lower down the socio-economic ladder one looks. And as wealthy students increasingly migrate to private schools, underprivileged kids become a bigger percentage of public-school students. The National Center for Education Statistics explained in 2018 that "more than 50% of the public-school population in the United States was made up of low-income students. This is a significant increase from 38% in 2001." When underprivileged kids struggle in school—surprise, surprise—their job prospects as adults suffer. And studies reveal that low-income students perform worse than wealthier students on average, as family wealth correlates strongly with academic success.[87]

America's schools (public and private combined) now compare very badly with the rest of the world. "Thirty countries now outperform the United States in mathematics at the high school level," *Education Week* explained in 2021. "Many are ahead in science, too. According to the Organization for Economic Co-operation and Development, the millennials in our workforce tied for last on tests of mathematics and problem solving among the millennials in the workforces of all the industrial countries tested. We now have the worst-educated workforce in the industrialized world. Because our workers are among the most highly paid in the world, that makes a lot of Americans uncompetitive in the global economy. And uncompetitive against increasingly smart machines. It is a formula for a grim future."

Worse still, America has saddled its young people with *$1.7 trillion* in student-loan debt. Skyrocketing tuition fees and government-sanctioned easy money have been a disastrous combination. To put it bluntly: the twenty-first century has been an economic catastrophe for America's college students and recent graduates. "Student debt has more than doubled over the last two decades," the Council on Foreign Relations explained. "As of September 2022, about forty-eight million U.S. borrowers collectively owed more than $1.6 trillion in federal student loans. Additional private loans bring that total to above $1.7 trillion, surpassing auto loans and credit card debt. Only home mortgage debt, at about $12 trillion, is larger." It's hard to think of a more destructive way to burden an entire generation and stymie their prospects than to weigh them down with crushing debt. This insanity doesn't just materially degrade the quality of their daily lives. It limits their ability to take risks, to innovate, and to give back to society.

America's public-education system does have some positive aspects. Many public schools do exemplary work. The majority of teachers perform admirably despite being underpaid. And most elite public universities are still leading educational institutions globally. The upper echelon of American public education is, indeed, unrivaled. But these discrete examples of high performance make it all the harder to swallow the unforgivable deficiencies. America shows its potential to excel in education; yet for so many of its young people, it fails miserably.

Adams and Jefferson would be appalled.

IMMIGRATION

America has long been "a proud nation of immigrants." This has been central to America's national identity—that it's a welcoming, meritocratic, and inclusive nation unconcerned with national origin and instead focused on democratic ideals. As Pew Research highlighted in August 2020, "The United States has more immigrants than any other country in the world. Today, more than 40 million people living in the U.S. were born in another country, accounting for about one-fifth of the world's migrants."

Unsurprisingly, this level of immigration has produced complex policy challenges. Yet the federal government hasn't passed comprehensive immigration legislation since 1986, when Ronald Reagan was president.[88] George W. Bush tried (and failed) during his presidency. And Barack Obama tried (and failed) too. One result of this governmental stasis is a porous southern border that's impossible to control. The legislative void, moreover, forces presidents to play whack-a-mole with aggressive, ineffective, and ad hoc executive actions. This breeds tension between the executive branch and the courts, and confusion between federal, state, and local authorities. And overcrowded court dockets clog the system as millions of pending federal immigration cases, before a few hundred judges, take years on average to resolve.[89] As a result, 10.5 million people live in America without lawful status, with the average length of unlawful residency a head-spinning fifteen years.[90]

The whole thing is a mess.

In recent years, hostility toward immigrants has increased—especially from Republicans. The anger among the white working class about globalization and inequality is often directed at undocumented immigrants, who are allegedly taking jobs away from American citizens. Donald Trump, who complained that many immigrants should go back to their "shithole countries," has used these sentiments to whip his base into a tribal frenzy. He has pushed one harsh, anti-immigrant initiative after another. Beginning during his first presidential campaign in 2015, Trump:

- Promised (and failed) to build a wall between the US and Mexico.
- Promised (and failed) to ban Muslims from entering the United States.
- Issued "over 400 executive actions directly targeting immigration and immigrants of all backgrounds."[91]
- Reduced the "number of admitted refugees to the United States to its lowest level in 40 years."[92]

- Restricted the "issuance of green cards and work visas for highly skilled individuals."[93]
- Separated thousands of children from their families at the southern border.
- Tried (and failed) to end the wildly popular and humane Deferred Action for Childhood Arrivals program.
- Tried (and failed) to withhold federal grants from so-called sanctuary cities, which protect immigrants from harsh federal laws.

Trump's approach to immigration was summed up nicely by the federal judge who struck down his administration's program separating families at the border. The administration's conduct was "so egregious, so outrageous, that it may fairly be said to shock the contemporary conscience" and "so 'brutal' and 'offensive' that it [does] not comport with traditional ideas of fair play and decency." And Trump's disdain for asylum seekers—often women and children fleeing horrific violence—was so extreme that America's asylum officers called Trump's Migrant Protection Protocols, which forced migrants to wait in perilous conditions in Mexico, "fundamentally contrary to the moral fabric of our Nation" and a "violation of international treaty and domestic legal obligations."

President Biden has tried to reverse many of Trump's draconian immigration policies. According to Pew Research, "Since President Joe Biden took office in January 2021, his administration has acted on a number of fronts to reverse Trump-era restrictions on immigration to the United States. The steps include plans to boost refugee admissions, preserving deportation relief for unauthorized immigrants who came to the U.S. as children and not enforcing the 'public charge' rule that denies green cards to immigrants who might use public benefits like Medicaid."

Many on the left, however, are concerned Biden hasn't done enough. The National Immigration Forum (NIF), for example, thinks the Biden administration "has often been unable to adhere to its initial, vocal commitments to protect the most vulnerable and has struggled to deliver on other elements of an ambitious immigration agenda." According to the NIF, moreover, "President Biden has at times failed to act decisively to protect asylum seekers, refugees, and others seeking humanitarian protection."

Exemplifying the tribal hysteria in this space, Biden has also been excoriated from the right. In a typical diatribe, Fox News host Sean Hannity put it this way: "The Biden administration now has completely dissolved our southern border. It no longer exists in this country. Whether his feeble mind realizes this or not, Joe Biden is now not only violating the law and violating his oath to the Constitution, he's now officially endangering the national security of this country."

It's impossible to get everything right with immigration. The problems are too large and too complicated. The key is to best harmonize three basic premises. First, every human life is equal. The system must value the life of every migrant just as much as the life of every American. Second, duly enacted immigration laws should be coherent and consistent. A system without clarity and predictability will generate substantial dysfunction. And third, the laws should be enforced. Intelligent control over international borders is a precondition to national stability and cohesion.

With these essential considerations in mind, America should have liberal and humane immigration laws. The government should offer a clear and practical path to citizenship to its millions of undocumented immigrants. The specter of deportation should be removed, allowing people and their families to invest in the future with confidence. The arbitrary limit on H-1B visas for high-skilled foreign workers—essential contributors in today's global economy—should be eliminated. And a generous asylum system should protect those in need, and default in favor of inclusion.

Having an elegant and smooth-running immigration system in a large, wealthy country that sits above a region riddled with hardship is downright impossible. But America can do so much better. And this challenge is also an opportunity: immigration reform is a chance to double down on America's ideals of inclusion and equality—and to show the nation can still be compassionate and competent.

THE ENVIRONMENT

A 2018 federal report put it plainly: "Earth's climate is now changing faster than at any point in the history of modern civilization, primarily as a result of human activities."[94] But words alone don't help. Action is what matters: "The impacts of global climate change are already being felt in the United States and are projected to intensify in the future—but the severity of future impacts will depend largely on actions taken to reduce greenhouse gas emissions and to adapt to the changes that will occur."

These conclusions are neither novel nor controversial. In most quarters the debate about climate change is over.[95] One of the few places it isn't, however, is a very influential one: the Republican Party in the United States of America. According to the party's champion, Donald Trump, for example, "The ice caps were going to melt, they were going to be gone by now, but now they're setting records, OK? They're at a record level." Technically he's right: as explained by NASA, Arctic Sea ice has been *declining* at a record level.[96] Republican presidential candidate Vivek Ramaswamy, moreover, expressed common tribal sentiments to an adoring crowd at the August 2023 Republican presidential debate: "The climate change agenda is a hoax ... The reality is more people are dying of bad climate change policies than they are of actual climate change."

But Republicans don't just mock and downplay climate change with their rhetoric. They follow it up with action. Trump withdrew America from the Paris Climate Accord, a broad international effort to cut harmful emissions. While the Paris Accord had its flaws, Trump's withdrawal was disastrous given the desperate need for global leadership and co-operation in this arena. His administration, moreover, dismantled a wide array of domestic climate regulations. According to *The Hill*, Trump staffed his administration "with climate change skeptics, including former Environmental Protection Agency Administrators Scott Pruitt and Andrew Wheeler, and unwound more than 100 existing environmental regulations while in office."

The Republicans' anti-environment movement storms ahead with Trump on the sidelines and Biden actively trying to address the problem. According to *Roll Call*, "At least four of the fiscal 2024 House Appropriations bills released so far propose to rescind some funding included in the IRA, including a big chunk of a $27 billion Greenhouse Gas Reduction Fund established at the EPA." These rescissions, "targeted at the administration's landmark effort to spend nearly $370 billion to address climate change, have drawn the ire of environmentalists." There is even an overarching Republican plan, called Project 2025—the year Republicans want to take back the presidency—that would, according to *Politico*, "block the expansion of the electrical grid for wind and solar energy; slash funding for the Environmental Protection Agency's environmental justice office; shutter the Energy Department's renewable energy offices; prevent states from adopting California's car pollution standards; and delegate more regulation of polluting industries to Republican state officials."

These actions would undercut the Biden administration's vital work on climate change and thwart the essential transition to clean energy that is now underway.[97] Republicans are laser-focused: "Project 2025 is not a white paper. We are not tinkering at the edges. We are writing a battle plan, and we are marshaling our forces," said Paul Dans, director of Project 2025 at the Heritage Foundation. "Never before has the whole conservative movement banded together to systematically prepare to take power day one and deconstruct the administrative state."

In 2022 the Supreme Court cleared a broad pathway for Republicans to achieve many of these goals. In a 6–3 decision—conservatives versus liberals, of course—the court ruled in favor of Republican-led states and curtailed the Environmental Protection Agency's ability to regulate greenhouse gases.[98]

Rooting its decision in the separation of powers, the court reasoned that the EPA had exceeded its statutory authority by requiring utilities to abandon coal power and move to clean energy.

As usual with highly political debates, many on the issue's right side are taking the wrong approach with their rhetoric. Progressives have produced a long list of counterproductive, overhyped predictions and exaggerations about climate change. For example, in a poster board for unhelpful assertions, New York Congresswoman Alexandria Ocasio-Cortez, a Democrat, said in January 2019, "The world is going to end in 12 years if we don't address climate change."

Oh my.

Statements like this have the exact *opposite* effect to what is intended: they help Republicans *downplay* the threat of climate change. Instead of arguing about climate change on the merits—where they always lose—Republicans can instead point out the absurdity of these statements, sow distrust among their constituents, and assert that climate change is a hoax. Case in point: Wisconsin Senator Ron Johnson, a Republican: "Without global warming, my state of Wisconsin would still be mostly covered by a 1–2-mile thick glacier," Johnson said in April 2023. "We should also stop scaring our children—and all of society for that matter—by predicting the world is about to end. It's not."

These policy failures are America's most consequential. But there are others. America's health-care system provides highly uneven services to rich and poor; fails to insure millions; and consumes an ever-increasing share of the nation's GDP.[99,100] Drug overdoses ravage communities from coast to coast, causing about 100,000 deaths (more than the Vietnam War) in both 2021 and 2022.[101] Older Americans are consistently left unprotected from scams and abuse.[102] Excessive red tape hampers small-business formation and success.[103] And America's infrastructure (roads, bridges, airports) is still a global embarrassment despite recent efforts to improve this.[104]

All these failures have a predictable consequence: Americans are losing trust in their government. As Gallup explained in 2022, polls over recent decades reveal that faith in government is plummeting: "Americans continue to lack faith in the federal government, with low levels of trust in all three branches. Gallup previously reported that trust in the judicial branch of the federal government has cratered in the past two years; it now sits at 47%, below the majority level for the first time in Gallup's polling history. At 43%, trust in the executive branch is just three percentage points above its record low from the Watergate era. Americans are even less trusting in the legislative branch, at 38%." The trend line is striking: "As recently as 2005, all three branches were trusted by majorities of Americans. And when Gallup first measured federal trust in 1972, no fewer than two-thirds trusted in each branch of the government."

A nation with America's wealth and maturity shouldn't tolerate a single major public-policy failure. The fact that the United States allows many to persist at once compels an unfortunate yet unavoidable conclusion: America isn't working.

9

Threats

"Those who cast the votes decide nothing. Those who count the votes decide everything"
Attributed to Josef Stalin

A large and diverse nation will always struggle with political dysfunction and public-policy failure—to some degree at least. But the extent and speed of America's descent this century is staggering. Tribal prejudices, juiced by social-media algorithms and two-party rivalries, have caused many Americans to cast aside the Constitutional principles and essential traditions that make the country work—all in pursuit of winning, at any cost, whatever myopic partisan fracas they're mired in today. This delirium is culminating in the two biggest threats to the American experiment's continuing viability: criminalizing politics and attacking elections.

CRIMINALIZING POLITICS
The indispensable line between politics and criminal justice is disintegrating. Politicians, pundits, and ordinary

people—from both sides of the tribal divide—increasingly want their political opponents prosecuted. Winning elections, legislative victories, and hearts and minds is no longer enough. Americans now long to see their fellow citizens behind bars. More and more, prosecutors oblige—bringing cases because of one's political affiliation rather than one's guilt or innocence. This dangerously undermines not just the rule of law, but the nation as a whole.

Both Joe Biden and Donald Trump are embroiled in numerous serious criminal matters. The DOJ is investigating Biden's son Hunter for his questionable business practices and has indicted him on tax charges and for lying on a gun application. The DOJ is also investigating Joe for his handling of classified government documents. And the Republicans have opened an impeachment inquiry into Joe's involvement in Hunter's business machinations, broadly investigating whether the president has committed an impeachable "high crime or misdemeanor" under the Constitution.

Trump is in much hotter water. He's been indicted four times (so far). In New York, prosecutors accuse him of creating fraudulent business documents to pay hush money to porn star Stormy Daniels, with whom he had an affair.[105] In Georgia, prosecutors accuse him of attempting to reverse that state's 2020-presidential-election results.[106] In Florida, the DOJ accuses him of stealing and refusing to return highly classified national-security documents.[107] And in Washington DC, the DOJ accuses him of broadly trying to overthrow the 2020 presidential election.[108]

While these are the most high-profile examples of politicians feeling the criminal law's heat, many others have, too. The list of American politicians who've been found guilty of a crime this century is long and growing:

- Scooter Libby (Chief of Staff to Vice President Dick Cheney) was convicted of perjury and obstruction of justice in 2007. Trump pardoned him in 2018.
- Ted Stevens (Republican Senator from Alaska) was convicted of hiding gifts in 2008.
- Robert E. Coughlin (Deputy Chief of Staff of the DOJ's Criminal Division under George W. Bush) pleaded guilty in 2009 to accepting bribes from lobbyist Jack Abramoff.
- William J. Jefferson (Democratic Congressman from Louisiana) was convicted for bribery in 2009.
- Jesse Jackson Jr. (Democratic Congressman from Illinois) pleaded guilty in 2013 to misusing $750,000 in campaign funds.
- David Petraeus (military general and Barack Obama's CIA Director) pleaded guilty in 2015 to providing classified information to a woman with whom he had an extramarital affair.
- Michael Flynn (Trump's National Security Advisor) pleaded guilty to lying to the FBI in 2017. Trump pardoned him in 2020.
- Roger Stone (Trump's political advisor) was convicted of obstructing justice in 2019. Trump commuted his sentence in 2020.
- Steve Bannon (Trump's White House Chief Strategist and Senior Counselor) was convicted in 2022 for failing to co-operate with the United States House Select Committee on the January 6 Attack.

- George Santos (Republican Congressman from New York) was indicted in 2023 for charging his donors' credit cards without authorization.
- Bob Menendez (Democratic Senator from New Jersey) was indicted in 2023 for bribery.

Some of these cases represent legitimate law-enforcement work. Some don't. But the problem is much bigger than just actual cases. Trump's 2016 campaign rallies saw thundering chants from the crowd of "lock her up," referring to his Democratic opponent Hillary Clinton. While president, Trump openly pressured the DOJ to prosecute his political rivals, including Hillary Clinton, Biden, Barack Obama, James Comey, and Andrew McCabe. Calls from Democrats to prosecute Trump and his loyalists, meanwhile, have been ubiquitous since 2016 (as have giddy celebrations when prosecutors do so). Even those who've investigated Trump's wrongdoing feel the heat. In 2022, former Republican Speaker of the House Newt Gingrich said that members of United States House Select Committee on the January 6 Attack would go to jail if Republicans took over the House of Representatives. Liz Cheney, a Republican member of the committee, responded: "A former Speaker of the House is threatening jail time for members of Congress who are investigating the violent January 6 attack on our Capitol and our Constitution. This is what it looks like when the rule of law unravels." And America's social-media platforms are constantly riven with exploding viral assertions that one political figure or another must go to jail.

Millions of Americans cheer or boo depending on who's in the crosshairs. But this isn't sport. It's a high-stakes game with the government's integrity and stability on the line. Political differences should be settled at the ballot box, not in the courtroom.

While some cases are necessary to bring, the pervasive tribal lust to prosecute political rivals is very dangerous. First, mixing the criminal law with tribal passions makes defendants' politics the focus, not their guilt or innocence. The political obsession with the messenger (as opposed to the message) and the actor (as opposed to the action) is fundamentally at odds with the rule of law's central tenet—that everyone is inherently equal under the law and only a defendant's specific alleged misdeeds are relevant.

Second, criminalizing politics turbocharges already disturbing levels of tribalism. Polarization's knife has already penetrated deep inside the body politic. Criminalizing politics twists it violently. Instead of treating political opponents like competitive rivals, they're treated like sworn enemies. Fierce domestic politics is hardly new, of course. It's woven into the fabric of America's two-party political system. But ultimately, America is one nation in a treacherous world. Scorched-earth domestic political disputes shouldn't consume too much national bandwidth. Nor should they reach such fervor as to undermine international diplomacy and national defense. When Democrats wrongfully accused Donald Trump of colluding with Russia to hack into the DNC's email servers, the hysteria undermined his administration's diplomacy with Russia for years. And the incessant Republican assertions that Joe Biden and his family were involved in Ukrainian corruption have been a petty yet meaningful distraction during the Ukraine–Russia war.

America's political energy should be channeled into winning elections, governing effectively, and addressing the country's numerous public-policy failures—not sending political rivals to jail.

Criminalizing politics also deters talented people from serving the country. American government already has a serious personnel problem. Just look at the presidency. Donald Trump was grossly unfit to hold America's highest office. His successor, Joe Biden, is a welcome reversion toward (but not quite to) the mean. Now in his eighties, Biden is neither what he once was nor the best American for the job. The House of Representatives, moreover, is throbbing with underqualified mediocrities. Americans shouldn't further dissuade quality people from serving because imperfections or ambiguities in their past might be shoehorned into politically motivated criminal accusations. The downside for winning office should be losing the next election, not going to jail.

It's also true, of course, that entering the government should neither absolve someone from past crimes nor authorize them to commit new ones. And the rule of law requires prosecuting not just the weak and anonymous but also the powerful and famous.

So how, then, should these competing concerns be balanced? How should people think about a criminal case when a politician is in the crosshairs?

Several guiding principles must govern. For starters, the universal rules of criminal law must be honored. All defendants—irrespective of political affiliation—must be presumed innocent. And they should receive all the robust protections the law provides. This includes the Constitutional right to confront their accusers and the rule of lenity, which requires ambiguous statutes to be read in defendants' favor. At the same time, no American—from a regular citizen to the president—is above the law. Those who commit clear crimes can and should be prosecuted.

Moreover, in determining whether a crime was committed, the focus must be on the actions and not the actor. Prosecutors must perform objective, conscientious analyses regarding whether the admissible evidence meets each specific element in a criminal statute. If a prosecutor wouldn't bring a case against a normal citizen then the prosecutor shouldn't bring it against a politician. And vice versa: if a prosecutor wouldn't bring a case against a politician then the prosecutor shouldn't bring it against a normal citizen.

And, finally, prosecutors must recognize both their awesome power and their inherent fallibility. It's a hazardous combination. As former Attorney General and Supreme Court justice Robert Jackson said, "The prosecutor has more control over life, liberty, and reputation than any other person in America. His discretion is tremendous." Yet despite this awesome power, the prosecutor is just as vulnerable to tribalism, bias, and misjudgment as anyone else. Confirmation bias, for example, can cause prosecutors to interpret (and often misinterpret) new evidence as consistent with pre-existing prejudices. There should never be a prosecution (of Donald Trump, Hunter Biden, or anyone else) if the prosecutor has pre-existing animus, to any degree, toward the defendant.

One of the key problems with Robert Mueller's investigation into Trump's alleged collusion with Russia—brushed aside by those who wanted Trump's blood—was the appearance, and likely reality, that members of his team had such animus toward Trump.

Donald Trump's four criminal cases offer an instructive continuum for evaluating this framework. In New York, prosecutor Alvin Bragg's case is an egregious example of criminalizing politics. The day of Trump's arraignment, Bragg, a Democrat, strode to the podium and—with a straight face—proclaimed that, "As this office has done time and time again, we today uphold our solemn responsibility to ensure that everyone stands equal before the law."

The opposite was true. Reaching back to events from seven years earlier, Bragg's case makes a very aggressive and overreaching argument. The New York criminal statute at issue requires a defendant to (1) falsify business documents and (2) do so to cover up a separate crime. So Bragg asserts that Trump (1) falsified business documents and (2) did so to cover up the hush-money payments to Stormy Daniels, which violated federal election law.

Individuals should only be prosecuted for clear crimes. Without exception. But two things here are manifestly unclear. First, whether the hush-money payments violated federal election law to begin with. No other defendant has been charged under such a tortured reading of the federal statute. And second, whether the New York law can be predicated on an underlying federal crime, as opposed to an underlying New York state crime. State law crimes typically don't depend on a defendant committing federal offenses.

Prosecutors should not bring outdated cases stitched together by such nauseating legal acrobatics. Bragg is obviously focused more on the man—Trump—than his alleged misdeeds.

The biggest problem here is not unfairness to Donald Trump. We could all live with just that. No, the real concern is what comes next. There are thousands of local prosecutors in America. What if they pile on? Given the law's malleability, the extent of potential abuse is virtually limitless. What if a Republican district attorney in Delaware lies in wait for Biden's presidency to end? Perhaps that's already happening. What if other prosecutors—from the right and the left—start bending the law to go after presidential candidates from the other tribe? Running for president would become (or perhaps already is) a clear and present danger to one's liberty. No nation can long withstand such a specter perennially hovering over its head of state. In twenty-first-century America, where every partisan wrong must be met with greater opposite force, Bragg's opening salvo makes this terrifying prospect exponentially more likely.

In Georgia, Fulton County district attorney Fani Willis—also a Democrat—is prosecuting Trump for trying to overturn the state's 2020 presidential election. Trump's on tape arguably doing just that. On an hour-long January 2, 2021 conference call, Trump pressured Georgia's Republican Secretary of State, Brad Raffensperger, to rewrite the election results in his favor. After Trump, still the incumbent president, rambled off a series of falsehoods, Raffensperger countered: "Well, Mr. President, the challenge that you have is, the data you have is wrong." Trump responded: "So look. All I want to do is this. I just want to find 11,780 votes, which is one more than we have. Because we won the state." He continued: "There's no way I lost Georgia. There's no way. We won by hundreds of thousands of votes."

Willis's case is very different from Bragg's. Here Trump's wrongdoing is both clear and significant. As Bob Bauer, Obama's White House Counsel, put it after the tape became public: "We now have irrefutable proof of a president pressuring and threatening an official of his own party to get him to rescind a state's lawful, certified vote count and fabricate another in its place."

Unfortunately, Willis's case is far too broad. She indicted not just Trump, but eighteen others, in a sweeping charge under Georgia's Racketeer Influenced and Corrupt Organizations Act. There are a whopping forty-one criminal charges in total. And they sweep in lots of conduct that shouldn't be criminalized, as not every dimension of the Republican's post-election activity in Georgia was criminal. It's okay to investigate, protest, and stress test election results *within the rules*; you just can't try to fraudulently reverse the outcome.

A criminal case requires a scalpel, not a sledgehammer. A more narrowly tailored case focusing on just Trump (and perhaps a few others) would have been much better. Deterring good-faith election challenges, like Al Gore's in 2000, is a mistake.

In Florida, DOJ special counsel Jack Smith is charging Trump for mishandling highly sensitive and classified documents after leaving office. Smith's case sits comfortably on the other side of the continuum from Bragg's: it's completely justified.

Indeed, this one's easy.

While Trump should not have had the documents to begin with, mishandling classified documents is common. Mistakes happen. Upon receiving the government's demand to return the documents, Trump could have and should have followed the standard playbook: apologize; co-operate; fix it. True to form, he did the opposite: he doubled down; he refused to co-operate; he jerked the government around. He even ordered his staff to delete security-camera footage to cover up his crimes. Trump's spoliation of evidence reveals knowledge of his own guilt.

This offense is serious. Laws governing classified national-security documents must be enforced. But Trump's misconduct here isn't as significant as what he did in Georgia. Trying to overthrow an election is worse than stealing classified documents. And proportional punishment is a key element of the rule of law. Trump should be punished if the government proves its case in court. But for this offense—of mishandling classified documents—he shouldn't go to jail in the middle of a presidential election.

Finally, in Washington DC, Smith is also prosecuting Trump for his behavior surrounding the 2020 presidential election. The indictment summarizes Trump's brazen misconduct:

> The Defendant, Donald J. Trump, lost the 2020 presidential election. Despite having lost, the Defendant was determined to remain in power. So for more than two months following election day on November 3, 2020, the Defendant spread lies that there had been outcome-determinative fraud in

the election and that he had actually won. These claims were false, and the Defendant knew that they were false. But the Defendant repeated and widely disseminated them anyway—to make his knowingly false claims appear legitimate, create an intense national atmosphere of mistrust and anger, and erode public faith in the administration of the election.

This case isn't only proper; it isn't merely justified; and it isn't simply necessary. This case is essential. As we'll examine shortly, Donald Trump's malfeasance surrounding the 2020 presidential election was the worst behavior of any president (or former president) in American history. He attacked America's election system. And in the process, he likely broke the law.

Bringing this case against Trump has two overarching consequences. The first is positive: it vindicates the rule of law and sets the precedent that election results must be respected. Given the large movement among Republicans to undermine election integrity, nothing is more important to American democracy than deterring future attempts to reverse election results. The second is negative: this case further enflames the tribal anger of Trump's base, which has long believed American government, including the DOJ, is out to get their champion. It may actually help Trump at the polls in 2024.

As is so often true, even doing the right thing in response to Donald Trump's wrongdoing has profound negative repercussions.

Donald Trump's cases are, unfortunately, just one element of America's criminalized politics. And this particular expression of how America isn't working is more dangerous than most others. For criminalizing politics isn't just unfair. And it doesn't just destabilize the government. It's the logical and inevitable precursor to something much worse. The last step before political violence is having the government eliminate political opponents for you by imprisoning them. And the first step after political violence is war.

ATTACKING ELECTIONS

America's tribal biases, social-media platforms, and political structures have generated such mania that even the defining element of America's representative democracy—the vote itself— is under siege. Tens of millions of Republicans are embracing Donald Trump's "Big Lie" that he, not Joe Biden, won the 2020 presidential election. The predicament couldn't be more striking: one of America's two major political parties is coalescing around a deeply troubled man whose central platform—destroying the integrity of elections— fundamentally warps the American experiment.

It started long before the November 3, 2020 presidential election. Donald Trump's "Big Lie" isn't a *response* to election-day evidence of fraud. No, Trump's plan to undermine the election was highly premeditated and long in the works. America's 45th president embraced a hallmark of third-world dictators clinging to thrones in banana republics: irrespective of the facts, if he lost the election he was going to say it was rigged.

Fox News Sunday host Chris Wallace asked Trump months before the election, on July 19, 2020, whether he would honor the election's results. Trump responded that he'd "have to see" and "it depends." "I'm not going to just say yes. I'm not going to say no," he said. A few days later Trump doubled down: "With Universal Mail-In Voting (not Absentee Voting, which is good), 2020 will be the most INACCURATE & FRAUDULENT Election in history. It will be a great embarrassment to the USA." At an August 17 Wisconsin rally, Trump told an adoring crowd, "The only way we're going to lose this election is if the election is rigged, remember that. It's the only way we're going to lose this election." During his acceptance speech as the party's nominee at the August 24 Republican National Convention, he said, "The only way they can take this election away from us is if this is a rigged election." And at a September 13 Nevada campaign rally, he claimed, "The Democrats are trying to rig this election because that's the only way they're going to win."

The election occurred on November 3. Joe Biden won. And Trump segued to the second, post-election phase of his plan. On November 7, as Biden was broadly confirmed the winner, Trump tweeted: "I WON THIS ELECTION, BY A LOT!" He promised: "[T]his election is far from over." On November 15, he said that Biden "won because the Election was Rigged. NO VOTE WATCHERS OR OBSERVERS allowed, vote tabulated by a Radical Left privately owned company, Dominion, with a bad reputation & bum equipment that couldn't even qualify for Texas (which I won by a lot!), the Fake & Silent Media, & more!" In mid-December, after the Electoral College formally selected Biden, Trump continued: "This Fake Election can no longer stand. Get moving Republicans." In January, still in the White House, Trump asserted again that he was the real winner. "They cheated and they rigged our presidential election ... NO WAY WE LOST THIS ELECTION!"

It was all lies. As the non-partisan *Cook Political Report*'s Dave Wasserman explained, "The case for Trump having won the election is so preposterous that the only explanation is that the losing side does not like the results." Trump's Attorney General at the time, William Barr, said later, "[T]here was no stealing of the election through fraud. Which means, you know, that people who were not qualified to vote or didn't exist, their votes were counted, or good votes were subtracted. The votes reflected the decision of the people." The "evidence" that Trump cites, Barr continued, is "nonsense" and "just false."

Yet, as we've seen, Trump's lies were only one dimension of a multifaceted attempt to steal the election. He filed dozens of lawsuits, most of which lacked sufficient merit to proceed in court. He pressured federal and state officials to "find" votes and reverse the results. He told Department of Justice leaders to lie and "say the election was corrupt and leave the rest to me and the Republican Congressmen." He pushed state officials to torpedo the Constitution's Electoral College and manufacture fake slates of electors.

Put simply, the incumbent President of the United States did everything in his power to reverse an election he lost.

The threat was so stark that on January 3, 2021, all living former United States Secretaries of Defense warned Trump against involving the military in his coup attempt: "Efforts to involve the U.S. armed forces in resolving election disputes would take us into dangerous, unlawful and unconstitutional territory. Civilian and military officials who direct or carry out such measures would be accountable, including potentially facing criminal penalties, for the grave consequences of their actions on our republic."

Three days later, on January 6, 2021, Trump held the fateful rally several blocks from the United States Capitol as Congress and Mike Pence tried to certify Joe Biden's victory. As noted in Chapter 4, Trump said to his supporters: "We're going to walk down to the Capitol, and we're going to cheer on our brave senators and Congressmen and women, and we're probably not going to be cheering so much for some of them, because you'll never take back our country with weakness. You have to show strength, and you have to be strong." Trump also said, "I know that everyone here will soon be marching over to the Capitol building to peacefully and patriotically make your voices heard."

His supporters then stormed the Capitol, breached the perimeter, and ransacked the building. As the mob roamed the Capitol chanting, "Hang Mike Pence!" Trump tweeted a message about his vice-president; a man who, until that day, had long been his loyal deputy: "Mike Pence didn't have the courage to do what should have been done to protect our Country and our Constitution."

It was the biggest and most sinister temper tantrum in human history, as a single man tried in vain to negate an electoral system that 335 million people depend on to legitimize their democracy. Trump failed. But his attempt was a high crime against the entire nation. A presidential election is the only time Americans all vote on the same question. The presidential election's winner thus has the highest legitimacy the American government affords. Indeed, Article II of the Constitution vests all its power in the president: "The executive Power shall be vested in a President of the United States."

This legitimacy weighed in Trump's favor for four years, protecting him against an onslaught of attempts to harm and undermine his presidency. The people spoke in 2016, and Donald Trump was the duly elected president. But the people also spoke in 2020. Joe Biden won. And the same vital electoral legitimacy that protected Trump for four years after he won made his misconduct after he lost so destructive. Trump's efforts to overturn the election results—from the White House—jeopardized the threshold premise of American democracy: that the people choose their leaders in free and fair elections.

At first, Republican leaders rejected Trump's behavior. Longtime Trump loyalist Senator Lindsey Graham of South Carolina said a few hours after the riot on January 6 that "Trump and I, we've had a hell of a journey. I hate it to end this way … From my point of view, he's been a consequential president, but today, first thing you'll see. All I can say is count me out. Enough is enough." House Republican leader Kevin McCarthy said on January 13 that the "violent attack on the Capitol was undemocratic, un-American, and criminal." McCarthy added: "The president bears responsibility for Wednesday's attack on Congress by mob rioters." And Republican Senate Majority Leader Mitch McConnell said on the Senate floor on January 19: "The mob was fed lies. They were provoked by the president and other powerful people."

These sentiments were the only sane reaction to what Trump had done. For a fleeting moment, the response to

Trump's behavior from Republican leaders finally seemed, if not proportional, at least somewhat responsible. But as rank-and-file Republican support for Trump didn't wane, party leaders quickly reversed course. Without shame. Graham soon re-emerged as a leading Trump supporter. McCarthy flew to Trump's home in Florida just a few weeks after the riot. And McConnell simply kept quiet. Despite having tried to overthrow an election, Trump's grip on the leadership of the Republican party hadn't even paused.

Neither had his stream of lies. In an October 27, 2021 letter to the *Wall Street Journal*'s editors, for example, Trump made the following baseless claims (among many others) about the 2020 presidential election in Pennsylvania:

- "305,874 voters were removed from the rolls after the election on Nov. 3rd."
- There were "57,000 duplicate registrations."
- There were "39,911 people who were added to voter rolls while under 17 years of age."
- "17,000 mail-in ballots [were] sent to addresses outside of Pennsylvania."

The *Wall Street Journal*'s editors, aptly enough, called these claims "bananas." In March 2022, moreover, Trump said that "the ballot harvesting scam will go down as the biggest political scandal in history. It is totally determinative, and the Democrats are doing everything they can to stop the news from coming out. Republicans must be strong and unified in order to save our Country." In May 2023 he asserted that it was a "rigged and stolen" election, highlighting that he won more counties than Biden. Then he asserted falsely, "Nothing like this has ever happened before. Usually it's very equal, or—but the winner always had the most counties." (The presidential winner often does not win the most counties.) And in September 2023, Trump claimed in California, "No way we lose this state in a real election," even though he had lost the state to President Biden by nearly thirty percentage points.

Trump's sustained efforts to undermine the electoral system are deeply troubling. But the worst part of it all—the true shock and awe—is that he continues to be the undisputed leader of his party. Well over half of all Republicans support him to be their nominee for president in 2024.

Michael Luttig, a former federal appellate judge, summed up the situation: "The former president sought to overturn an American election which he had lost fair and square. For four years, these claims by the former president and his Republican allies have corroded and corrupted American democracy and American elections." The impact of Trump's behavior on his most loyal supporters, Luttig continued, has been profound: "Vast, vast numbers of Americans, into the millions, today no longer believe in the elections in the United States of America. They no longer believe in the institutions of law and democracy in America, the very pillars of our foundation. And many of those people have begun even to question the Constitution of the United States."

A common narrative among Democrats is that "those people"—Trump's core supporters—are detached from reality, that to them the facts don't matter. How else could they possibly support this lunatic's attempt to overthrow

American democracy? This narrative is far too simple. Many Trump supporters know exactly what he's doing. But for them causation has flipped upside-down: the *worse* Trump behaves, the *worse* the facts, the *more* they support him. But why? Why would this deranged dynamic be engulfing American politics? The answer makes the blood curdle: because many Republicans don't want the American experiment to succeed. Their populist anger and tribalism are so extraordinary that what they really want is to tear the system down.

These are the people, mainly from the white working class, who lost their jobs to a globalized economy. Whose towns were decimated. Whose pride was shattered. These are the people who Hillary Clinton said were "deplorables," who Barack Obama said were "bitter" and "cling to guns or religion or antipathy to people who aren't like them." These are the people who J. D. Vance explained are behind a growing movement that blames government elites (like Hillary Clinton and Barack Obama) for their profound personal disappointments. "The deeper, long-term reasons for today's rage are not hard to find," Andrew Sullivan wrote in 2016, as Trump was dominating the Republican party's presidential primary.

> The jobs available to the working class no longer contain the kind of craftsmanship or satisfaction or meaning that can take the sting out of their low and stagnant wages. The once-familiar avenues for socialization—the church, the union hall, the VFW [Veterans of Foreign Wars of the United States]—have become less vibrant and social isolation more common. Global economic forces have pummeled

blue-collar workers more relentlessly than almost any other segment of society, forcing them to compete against hundreds of millions of equally skilled workers throughout the planet. No one asked them in the 1990s if this was the future they wanted. And the impact has been more brutal than many economists predicted. No wonder suicide and mortality rates among the white working poor are spiking dramatically.

Indeed, you just have to listen to what these people say to understand why they support Donald Trump. Steve Bannon, for example, is an alt-right hero to the pro-Trump white working class. Bannon rose from Breitbart News editor to running Trump's victorious 2016 presidential campaign. From there he became Trump's White House Chief Strategist and Senior Counselor. His politics derive from his father's experience losing his life savings during the 2008 financial crisis. According to Bannon, the elites (inside and outside American government) who built the global capitalist system emerged from the wreckage unscathed—often even richer—while working-class heroes like his father were decimated. Bannon doesn't hide his intent: "Lenin wanted to destroy the state, and that's my goal too. I want to bring everything crashing down, and destroy all of today's establishment."

These sentiments, more than anything else, explain the Trump phenomenon. For what better vessel is there in the entire world for accomplishing this goal—for bringing everything crashing down—than Donald J. Trump?

That's why Trump's behavior in office was okay. That's why his lies about the election are just fine. That's why the

January 6 riot didn't matter. Not because Trump's base thinks those things are good for America … but because they know those things are bad for America.

Trump has come. And he will go. But what does it say about the underlying state of the American polity that a politician whose central platform is lying about elections is the unrivaled champion of one of the two major political parties? Something broad and deep is afoot. Something pernicious. Something likely to last.

10

The Future

"Science is more than a body of knowledge; it is a way of thinking. I have a foreboding of an America in my children's or grandchildren's time—when the United States is a service and information economy; when nearly all the key manufacturing industries have slipped away to other countries; when awesome technological powers are in the hands of a very few, and no one representing the public interest can even grasp the issues; when the people have lost the ability to set their own agendas or knowledgeably question those in authority; when, clutching our crystals and nervously consulting our horoscopes, our critical faculties in decline, unable to distinguish between what feels good and what's true, we slide, almost without noticing, back into superstition and darkness"

Carl Sagan (1995)

America's dysfunctions, failures, and threats raise fundamental questions about the future and whether America will start working again. Is America's twenty-first-century decline merely another dip in a long arc of non-linear, yet essentially upward, progress? Or is it, rather, the first phase of a steep and irreversible decline?

The answer, again, lies with the American people. Like all nations, America is, above all, the hearts and minds of its people. And as this book details, things are getting worse, not better. Tribalism is intensifying. Social-media platforms are getting smarter at manipulating human cognition. The US political system's defects are worsening. And America's public-policy failures are deepening.

The remedies are easy to prescribe. Americans must improve civic education in schools; raise awareness about cognitive biases throughout society; spend more time with people from other political tribes; reduce and regulate the use of social media; rework the political structure to foster more political parties and equal representation; double down on free speech; shun politically motivated prosecutions; feverishly guard election integrity; and support a new Republican champion other than Donald Trump.

Yet in practice these goals have so far been impossible to achieve.

And two broad and overlapping global trends will only make reversing the free fall harder as the twenty-first century marches on. First, technology is getting more sophisticated—at a dizzying pace. The positives are huge. The internet democratizes education. Streaming innovations like Netflix enrich entertainment. New products like self-driving cars will revolutionize transportation. Highly sophisticated research dramatically improves medicine. Pioneering technologies substantially broaden the distribution of necessities like food and clothing.

But the negatives are unnerving. Online innovations like deepfakes compound the internet's harms. Poor cybersecurity undermines the safety of personal data and the control of computerized systems. Popular applications like Chinese-owned TikTok give rival governments control over Americans' private information. Artificial intelligence jeopardizes humanity in ways not yet clear. Industrial innovations like fracking plunder the environment. Battlefield inventions like drones threaten to change the face of warfare.

Second, international affairs are getting more complicated. It took America a full two centuries to achieve global hegemony—and merely two decades to lose it. As former United States CIA Director and Defense Secretary Robert Gates wrote in a 2023 *Foreign Affairs* essay, *The Dysfunctional Superpower*, geopolitical threats to America are multiplying: "The United States finds itself in a uniquely treacherous position: facing aggressive adversaries with a propensity to miscalculate yet incapable of mustering the unity and strength necessary to dissuade them." According to Gates: "The United States now confronts graver threats to its security than it has in decades, perhaps ever. Never before has it faced four allied antagonists at the same time—Russia, China, North Korea, and Iran—whose collective nuclear arsenal could within a few years be nearly double the size of its own. Not since the Korean War has the United States had to contend with powerful military rivals in both Europe and Asia. And no one alive can remember a time when an adversary had as much economic, scientific, technological, and military power as China does today."

But it's not just America's biggest rivals that matter. Within a few decades, it's likely that even small countries will have military capacities that in key respects exceed those of the superpowers today. Given the dominance and cohesion of America's military, another civil war is highly unlikely. The worst-case scenario arising from America's dysfunction isn't domestic mismanagement; it's foreign policy miscalculation.

These dynamics establish a striking truism that looms over humanity: the world's pre-eminent democracy and most powerful nation is in decline precisely when the challenges faced by the world are mounting and its need for rational leadership has never been more urgent.

The American experiment has seen better days, certainly, but it's important to remember that it has also seen worse days. Today's struggles pale in comparison to the republic's early days when slavery and conquest predominated. No one would choose either the Civil War era or Reconstruction over contemporary America. And the wars of the twentieth century (both world wars, Korea, and Vietnam) were far more devastating than twenty-first-century America's worst conflagrations.

Somewhere beneath the thickening surface of tribal bedlam and political fervor, moreover, is still a core national impulse to confront and overcome big challenges. The question is how strong that impulse remains.

The French political scientist Alexis de Tocqueville visited America in 1831 and 1832. A close observer of human behavior, de Tocqueville traveled across the country taking copious notes on what he saw. His book *Democracy in America* is a classic text in American political science. And he's been revered for capturing the true essence of America like few others have, either before or since. Perhaps de Tocqueville's most profound insight was that the "greatness of America lies not in being more enlightened than any other nation, but rather in her ability to repair her faults." Twenty-first-century America is putting this thesis through a searing test. And the world will find out, soon enough, whether or not it's still true.

Appendices

APPENDIX 1

THE BILL OF RIGHTS

Preamble

Congress of the United States begun and held at the City of New-York, on Wednesday the fourth of March, one thousand seven hundred and eighty nine.

THE Conventions of a number of the States, having at the time of their adopting the Constitution, expressed a desire, in order to prevent misconstruction or abuse of its powers, that further declaratory and restrictive clauses should be added: And as extending the ground of public confidence in the Government, will best ensure the beneficent ends of its institution.

RESOLVED by the Senate and House of Representatives of the United States of America, in Congress assembled, two thirds of both Houses concurring, that the following

Articles be proposed to the Legislatures of the several States, as amendments to the Constitution of the United States, all, or any of which Articles, when ratified by three fourths of the said Legislatures, to be valid to all intents and purposes, as part of the said Constitution; viz.

ARTICLES in addition to, and Amendment of the Constitution of the United States of America, proposed by Congress, and ratified by the Legislatures of the several States, pursuant to the fifth Article of the original Constitution.

Amendment I

Congress shall make no law respecting an establishment of religion, or prohibiting the free exercise thereof; or abridging the freedom of speech, or of the press; or the right of the people peaceably to assemble, and to petition the Government for a redress of grievances.

Amendment II

A well regulated Militia, being necessary to the security of a free State, the right of the people to keep and bear Arms, shall not be infringed.

Amendment III

No Soldier shall, in time of peace be quartered in any house, without the consent of the Owner, nor in time of war, but in a manner to be prescribed by law.

Amendment IV

The right of the people to be secure in their persons, houses, papers, and effects, against unreasonable searches and seizures, shall not be violated, and no Warrants shall issue, but upon probable cause, supported by Oath or affirmation, and particularly describing the place to be searched, and the persons or things to be seized.

Amendment V

No person shall be held to answer for a capital, or otherwise infamous crime, unless on a presentment or indictment of a Grand Jury, except in cases arising in the land or naval forces, or in the Militia, when in actual service in time of War or public danger; nor shall any person be subject for the same offence to be twice put in jeopardy of life or limb; nor shall be compelled in any criminal case to be a witness against himself, nor be deprived of life, liberty, or property, without due process of law; nor shall private property be taken for public use, without just compensation.

Amendment VI

In all criminal prosecutions, the accused shall enjoy the right to a speedy and public trial, by an impartial jury of the State and district wherein the crime shall have been committed, which district shall have been previously ascertained by law, and to be informed of the nature and cause of the accusation; to be confronted with the witnesses against him; to have compulsory process for obtaining witnesses in his favor, and to have the Assistance of Counsel for his defence.

Amendment VII

In Suits at common law, where the value in controversy shall exceed twenty dollars, the right of trial by jury shall be preserved, and no fact tried by a jury, shall be otherwise re-examined in any Court of the United States, than according to the rules of the common law.

Amendment VIII
Excessive bail shall not be required, nor excessive fines imposed, nor cruel and unusual punishments inflicted.

Amendment IX
The enumeration in the Constitution, of certain rights, shall not be construed to deny or disparage others retained by the people.

Amendment X
The powers not delegated to the United States by the Constitution, nor prohibited by it to the States, are reserved to the States respectively, or to the people.

APPENDIX 2

Statement on Climate Change from 18 Scientific Associations
"Observations throughout the world make it clear that climate change is occurring, and rigorous scientific research demonstrates that the greenhouse gases emitted by human activities are the primary driver." (2009)

American Association for the Advancement of Science
"Based on well-established evidence, about 97% of climate scientists have concluded that human-caused climate change is happening." (2014)

American Chemical Society

"The Earth's climate is changing in response to increasing concentrations of greenhouse gases (GHGs) and particulate matter in the atmosphere, largely as the result of human activities." (2016–2019)

American Geophysical Union

"Based on extensive scientific evidence, it is extremely likely that human activities, especially emissions of greenhouse gases, are the dominant cause of the observed warming since the mid-20th century. There is no alterative explanation supported by convincing evidence." (2019)

American Medical Association

"Our AMA ... supports the findings of the Intergovernmental Panel on Climate Change's fourth assessment report and concurs with the scientific consensus that the Earth is undergoing adverse global climate change and that anthropogenic contributions are significant." (2019)

American Meteorological Society

"Research has found a human influence on the climate of the past several decades ... The IPCC (2013), USGCRP (2017), and USGCRP (2018) indicate that it is extremely likely that human influence has been the dominant cause of the observed warming since the mid-twentieth century." (2019)

American Physical Society

"Earth's changing climate is a critical issue and poses the risk of significant environmental, social and economic disruptions around the globe. While natural sources of climate variability are significant, multiple lines of evidence indicate that human influences have had an increasingly dominant effect on global climate warming observed since the mid-twentieth century." (2015)

The Geological Society of America
"The Geological Society of America (GSA) concurs with assessments by the National Academies of Science (2005), the National Research Council (2011), the Intergovernmental Panel on Climate Change (IPCC, 2013) and the U.S. Global Change Research Program (Melillo et al., 2014) that global climate has warmed in response to increasing concentrations of carbon dioxide (CO_2) and other greenhouse gases ... Human activities (mainly greenhouse-gas emissions) are the dominant cause of the rapid warming since the middle 1900s (IPCC, 2013)." (2015)

Acknowledgments

I'd first like to thank Duncan Proudfoot, Mel Sambells, Kaz Harrison, and the team at Gemini Adult Books in London for their wise counsel and strong partnership. It's been a true privilege to work with Gemini's exceptional roster of talented publishing professionals.

Stateside, Lissa Warren's passion for and expertise in book publicity—a powerful combination—has been extraordinary. Author Michael McKinley's wisdom, advice, and friendship have been invaluable. Erik Fleming, moreover, doesn't just host the best political podcast in the world. He's also a deeply intelligent and wise thinker about America and why it isn't working.

I'm also grateful to the many journalists, authors, and scholars who took time to connect with me on this project, including Ed Larson, Robert Shapiro, Robert Legvold, Anthony Fowler, Michael Allen Gillespie, Jacob Smith, Richard Albert, Shannon O'Brien, Ray Madoff, Zygmunt Plater, John Knox, and Barry McDonald.

ACKNOWLEDGMENTS

And finally, I'd like to thank my critics—at the *New Republic* and *Jacobin* magazine; on the editorial pages of the *Tampa Bay Times*, South Florida *Sun Sentinel*, and *San Francisco Chronicle*; in the Twittersphere, the blogosphere, and elsewhere—for giving me an opportunity to heed my own advice on disconfirming evidence (Chapter 6) and consider closely their critiques, not all of which are without merit.

Endnotes

1. https://www.cambridge.org/core/books/
   the-cambridge-world-history-of-violence/
   C244F0BAAC47E99EBC1110AF6293D9D7
2. https://ourworldindata.org/war-and-peace
3. https://slaveryandjusticereport.brown.edu/sections/slavery-
   the-slave-trade-and-brown/#:~:text=The%20oldest%20
   surviving%20system%20of,in%20the%20antebellum%20
   American%20South.
4. https://www.abhmuseum.org/how-many-africans-were-
   really-taken-to-the-u-s-during-the-slave-trade/
5. https://www.mckinsey.com/mhi/our-insights/adding-years-
   to-life-and-life-to-years
6. https://education.nationalgeographic.org/resource/
   roman-republic/
7. https://www.archives.gov/milestone-documents/articles-
   of-confederation
8. https://Constitutioncenter.org/blog/on-this-day-shays-
   rebellion-starts-in-massachusetts
9. https://Constitution.Congress.gov/

10. https://claremontreviewofbooks.com/three-fifths-historian/#:~:text=Wills%20calculates%20that%2C%20in%20a,a%20margin%20of%2065%2D61.

11. For the full text of the Bill of Rights see Appendix 1 on p. 191.

12. https://tile.loc.gov/storage-services/service/ll/usrep/usrep554/usrep554570/usrep554570.pdf

13. https://www.supremecourt.gov/opinions/21pdf/20-843_7j80.pdf

14. https://www.pbs.org/newshour/health/theres-a-new-global-ranking-of-gun-deaths-heres-where-the-u-s-stands

15. https://www.whitehouse.gov/about-the-white-house/our-government/the-Constitution/#:~:text=An%20amendment%20may%20be%20proposed,in%20each%20State%20for%20ratification

16. https://www.washingtonpost.com/news/volokh-conspiracy/wp/2017/11/07/lessons-from-a-century-of-communism/

17. https://www.supremecourt.gov/opinions/22pdf/22-506_nmip.pdf

18. https://www.supremecourt.gov/opinions/21pdf/20-1530_n758.pdf

19. https://www.washingtonpost.com/wp-srv/politics/special/clinton/icreport/icreport.htm

20. https://www.washingtonpost.com/archive/politics/2000/04/01/52-million-starr-probe-costliest-ever/3be88582-f0ee-4673-ac0c-f66c87326e82/

21. https://www.nytimes.com/2019/12/18/us/politics/trump-impeached.html

22. full text: "The President, Vice President and all civil Officers of the United States, shall be removed from Office on Impeachment for, and Conviction of, Treason, Bribery, or other high Crimes and Misdemeanors."

23. https://www.senate.gov/about/powers-procedures/impeachment.htm#:~:text=The%20Constitution%20requires%20a%20two,There%20is%20no%20appeal.
24. https://www.scotusblog.com/2021/03/court-dismisses-sanctuary-cities-petitions/
25. https://nepc.colorado.edu/blog/federally-mandated
26. The court ruled: "Segregation of white and colored children in public schools has a detrimental effect upon the colored children … We conclude that in the field of public education the doctrine of 'separate but equal' has no place. Separate educational facilities are inherently unequal."
27. https://www.archives.gov/milestone-documents/voting-rights-act
28. The full text of the 1st Amendment: "Congress shall make no law respecting an establishment of religion, or prohibiting the free exercise thereof; or abridging the freedom of speech, or of the press; or the right of the people peaceably to assemble, and to petition the Government for a redress of grievances."
29. https://www.jan-6.com/_files/ugd/2cf5f9_e0790657e2dc4bc2bd8675069a6e7911.pdf
30. https://www.cato.org/survey-reports/state-free-speech-tolerance-america
31. https://gizmodo.com/exclusive-heres-the-full-10-page-anti-diversity-screed-1797564320
32. https://www.dailymail.co.uk/news/article-9193103/San-Francisco-school-board-votes-rename-schools.html
33. https://www.ncbi.nlm.nih.gov/pmc/articles/PMC7343248/
34. https://www.loc.gov/exhibits/creating-the-united-states/formation-of-political-parties.html
35. CQ Press Guide to U.S. Political Parties (June 2014)

36. https://www.presidency.ucsb.edu/statistics/elections/1992

37. https://www.fec.gov/documents/1614/2000ptables.xls

38. https://www.oyez.org/cases/1789-1850/5us137

39. Article III, Section 1: "The judicial Power of the United States, shall be vested in one Supreme Court, and in such inferior Courts as the Congress may from time to time ordain and establish. The Judges, both of the supreme and inferior Courts, shall hold their Offices during good Behaviour, and shall, at stated Times, receive for their Services, a Compensation, which shall not be diminished during their Continuance in Office."

40. https://www.archives.gov/milestone-documents/dred-scott-v-sandford

41. https://www.archives.gov/milestone-documents/plessy-v-ferguson

42. https://www.oyez.org/cases/1900-1940/198us45

43. https://www.oyez.org/cases/1940-1955/323us214

44. https://www.oyez.org/cases/2000/00-949

45. https://www.senate.gov/legislative/LIS/roll_call_votes/vote1152/vote_115_2_00223.htm

46. https://www.supremecourt.gov/opinions/21pdf/19-1392_6j37.pdf

47. https://www.supremecourt.gov/opinions/21pdf/20-843_7j80.pdf

48. https://www.bls.gov/opub/mlr/2015/article/labor-law-highlights-1915-2015.htm

49. https://www.dol.gov/agencies/ilab/reports/child-labor/list-of-goods

50. https://www.nytimes.com/2022/04/07/magazine/billionaires.html

51. https://inequality.org/great-divide/updates-billionaire-pandemic/

52. https://www.oecd.org/trade/topics/trade-and-the-environment/

53. https://www.un.org/millenniumgoals/poverty.shtml
54. https://world101.cfr.org/global-era-issues/development/two-koreas-two-development-policies-0
55. https://www.forbes.com/sites/mikepatton/2016/02/29/u-s-role-in-global-economy-declines-nearly-50/?sh=627a06635e9e
56. https://ourworldindata.org/war-and-peace
57. https://ourworldindata.org/extreme-poverty-in-brief
58. https://ourworldindata.org/literacy
59. https://ourworldindata.org/life-expectancy
60. https://www.pewresearch.org/short-reads/2019/02/13/8-facts-about-love-and-marriage/
61. https://www.nytimes.com/interactive/2017/11/14/upshot/climate-change-by-education.html
62. https://pmarca.substack.com/p/availability-cascades-run-the-world
63. https://www.cnn.com/politics/live-news/trump-tower-meeting-transcripts/h_040fc12f0f89b766143e2fdada711 05f
64. https://www.aeaweb.org/conference/2010/retrieve.php?pdfid=401
65. https://www.loc.gov/ghe/cascade/index.html?appid=580eda c150234258a49a3eeb58d9121c
66. Rebranded as merely X in 2023.
67. Garrett, R. K. et al. Implications of pro- and counterattitudinal information exposure for affective polarization: Partisan media exposure and affective polarization. Hum. Commun. Res. 40, 309–332 (2014).
68. Lu, Y. & Lee, J.K. Partisan information sources and affective polarization: panel analysis of the mediating role of anger and fear. Journal. Mass Commun. Q 96, 767–783 (2019).
69. https://www.ncbi.nlm.nih.gov/pmc/articles/PMC8853081/

70. https://www.nytimes.com/2021/07/31/opinion/smartphone-iphone-social-media-isolation.html
71. https://www.science.org/doi/10.1126/science.abe1715
72. https://www.ncsl.org/elections-and-campaigns/state-primary-election-types
73. https://www.americanprogress.org/article/impact-partisan-gerrymandering/
74. https://pubmed.ncbi.nlm.nih.gov/14599246/
75. https://www.dol.gov/agencies/oasam/civil-rights-center/statutes/civil-rights-act-of-1964
76. https://www.annenbergpublicpolicycenter.org/political-communication/civics-knowledge-survey/
77. "Congress shall make no law respecting an establishment of religion, or prohibiting the free exercise thereof; or abridging the freedom of speech, or of the press; or the right of the people peaceably to assemble, and to petition the Government for a redress of grievances."
78. https://www.nytimes.com/2021/09/27/us/fbi-murders-2020-cities.html
79. https://www.wsj.com/articles/the-murder-spike-of-2020-when-police-pull-back-11626969547
80. https://www.nasdaq.com/articles/the-worlds-5-smallest-economies
81. https://www.nlihc.org/resource/hud-2022-annual-homeless-assessment-report-finds-unsheltered-homelessness-rise#:~:text=HUD%20has%20released%20the%202022,3%25%20increase%20from%202020.
82. https://www.oxfam.org/en/press-releases/richest-1-bag-nearly-twice-much-wealth-rest-world-put-together-over-past-two-years
83. https://www.imf.org/external/pubs/ft/issues11/

84. https://nces.ed.gov/fastfacts/display.asp?id=55#:~:text=
Overall%2C%2053.9%20million%20K%E2%80%9312,
were%20enrolled%20in%20public%20schools.
85. https://nces.ed.gov/fastfacts/display.asp?id=372
86. https://nces.ed.gov/pubs2018/2018095.pdf
87. https://inequality.stanford.edu/sites/default/files/
PathwaysWinter11_Evans.pdf
88. https://www.brookings.edu/articles/
can-immigration-reform-happen-a-look-back/
89. https://humanrightsfirst.org/wp-content/uploads/2022/10/
HRF-Court-Backlog-Brief.pdf
90. https://www.pewresearch.org/short-reads/2019/06/12/5-
facts-about-illegal-immigration-in-the-u-s/
91. https://www.brookings.edu/articles/the-road-to-fix-
americas-broken-immigration-system-begins-abroad/
92. Id.
93. Id.
94. Fourth National Climate Assessment: Volume II (2018)
95. For the 'Statement on Climate Change from 18 Scientific
Associations' see Appendix 2 on p. 194.
96. https://climate.nasa.gov/news/3284/arctic-sea-ice-
6th-lowest-on-record-antarctic-sees-record-low-
growth/#:~:text=These%20both%20continue%20a%20
long,Ice%20Data%20Center%20(NSIDC).
97. https://www.whitehouse.gov/briefing-room/
statements-releases/2023/04/20/fact-sheet-president-biden-
to-catalyze-global-climate-action-through-the-major-
economies-forum-on-energy-and-climate/
98. https://www.supremecourt.gov/opinions/21pdf/20-1530_
n758.pdf
99. https://www.ncbi.nlm.nih.gov/pmc/articles/PMC8572548/

100. https://www.ncbi.nlm.nih.gov/pmc/articles/PMC5394555/
101. https://nida.nih.gov/research-topics/trends-statistics/
     overdose-death-rates#:~:text=There%20were%20
     106%2C699%20drug%2Dinvolved,to%202021%20
     (Figure%202).
102. https://www.ncoa.org/article/top-5-financial-scams-
     targeting-older-adults
103. https://www.govinfo.gov/content/pkg/CHRG-
     115hhrg26719/html/CHRG-115hhrg26719.htm
104. https://www.cfr.org/backgrounder/state-us-infrastructure
105. https://www.manhattanda.org/wp-content/uploads/
     2023/04/Donald-J.-Trump-Indictment.pdf
106. https://www.nytimes.com/live/2023/08/14/us/trump-
     indictment-georgia-election
107. https://www.justice.gov/storage/US_v_Trump-Nauta_
     23-80101.pdf
108. https://www.jan-6.com/_files/ugd/2cf5f9_e0790657e2d
     c4bc2bd8675069a6e7911.pdf

Bibliography

Alexander, Michelle: *The New Jim Crow: Mass Incarceration in the Age of Colorblindness* [The New Press, 2020]

Baime, A. J.: *The Accidental President: Harry S. Truman and the Four Months That Changed the World* [Mariner Books, 2017]

Barsamian, David; Chomsky, Noam: *Propaganda and the Public Mind* [South End Press, 2001]

Brennan, Jason: *Against Democracy* [Princeton, 2016]

Bush, George W.: *Decision Points* [Crown, 2010]

Chernow, Ron: *Alexander Hamilton* [Penguin, 2004]

Chernow, Ron: *Washington: A Life* [Penguin, 2011]

Chua, Amy: *Political Tribes: Group Instinct and the Fate of Nations* [Penguin Press, 2018]

Clinton, Bill: *My Life* [Knopf, 2004]

Cohen, Michael: *Disloyal: A Memoir: The True Story of the Former Personal Attorney to President Donald J. Trump* [Skyhorse, 2020]

Cooper, William: *Stress Test: How Donald Trump Threatens American Democracy* [Black Spring Press Group, 2022]

Coppins, McKay: *Romney: A Reckoning* [Scribner, 2023]

Dershowitz, Alan: *Get Trump: The Threat to Civil Liberties, Due Process, and Our Constitutional Rule of Law* [Hot Books, 2023]

Desmond, Matthew: *Evicted: Poverty and Profit in the American City* [Crown, 2017]

Desmond, Matthew: *Poverty, by America* [Crown, 2023]

Drutman, Lee: *Breaking the Two-Party Doom Loop: The Case for Multiparty Democracy in America* [Oxford, 2020]

Duke, Annie: *Thinking in Bets* [Portfolio, 2018]

Dunbar-Ortiz, Roxanne: *An Indigenous Peoples' History of the United States* [Beacon Press, 2015]

Foer, Franklin: *The Last Politician: Inside Joe Biden's White House and the Struggle for America's Future* [Penguin Press, 2023]

Freddoso, David: *The Case Against Barack Obama: The Unlikely Rise and Unexamined Agenda of the Media's Favorite Candidate* [Regnery, 2008]

Hanson, Victor Davis: *The Dying Citizen: How Progressive Elites, Tribalism, and Globalization Are Destroying the Idea of America* [Basic Books, 2021]

Herman, Edward S.; Chomsky, Noam: *Manufacturing Consent: The Political Economy of the Mass Media* [Pantheon, 1988]

Hochschild, Adam: *Bury the Chains: Prophets and Rebels in the Fight to Free an Empire's Slaves* [Houghton Mifflin Harcourt, 2005]

Hochschild, Adam: *King Leopold's Ghost: A Story of Greed, Terror, and Heroism in Colonial Africa* [Mariner Books, 1999]

Inskeep, Steve: *Differ We Must: How Lincoln Succeeded in a Divided America* [Penguin Press, 2023]

Kahneman, Daniel: *Thinking, Fast and Slow* [Farrar, Straus and Giroux, 2013]

Karl, Jonathan: *Tired of Winning: Donald Trump and the End of the Grand Old Party* [Dutton, 2023]

Keyssar, Alexander: *Why Do We Still Have the Electoral College?* [Harvard, 2022]

Kissinger, Henry: *Diplomacy* [Simon & Schuster, 1994]

Kissinger, Henry: *White House Years* [Simon & Schuster, 1980]

Klein, Ezra: *Why We're Polarized* [Avid Reader Press, 2021]

Krauthammer, Charles: *The Point of It All: A Lifetime of Great Loves and Endeavors* [Forum, 2018]

Krauthammer, Charles: *Things That Matter: Three Decades of Passions, Pastimes and Politics* [Forum, 2015]

Krugman, Paul: *The Conscience of a Liberal* [Norton, 2009]

Krugman, Paul: *The Great Unraveling: Losing Our Way in the New Century* [Norton, 2003]

Levin, Mark R.: *The Democrat Party Hates America* [Threshold Editions, 2023]

Levitsky, Steven; Ziblatt, Daniel: *How Democracies Die* [Crown, 2019]

Lewis, Anthony: *Gideon's Trumpet: How One Man, a Poor Prisoner, Took His Case to the Supreme Court—and Changed the Law of the United States* [Random House, 1964]

Locke, John: *Second Treatise of Government* [1690]

Loewen, James W.: *Lies My Teacher Told Me: Everything Your American History Textbook Got Wrong* [The New Press, 2018]

Maddow, Rachel; Yarvitz, Michael: Bag Man: *The Wild Crimes, Audacious Cover-up, and Spectacular Downfall of a Brazen Crook in the White House* [Crown, 2020]

Maddow, Rachel: *Prequel: An American Fight Against Fascism* [Crown, 2023]

Meacham, Jon: *American Lion: Andrew Jackson in the White House* [Random House, 2009]

Meacham, Jon: *And There Was Light: Abraham Lincoln and the American Struggle* [Random House, 2022]

Meacham, Jon: *Thomas Jefferson: The Art of Power* [Random House, 2013]

Miller, Chris: *Chip War: The Fight for the World's Most Critical Technology* [Scribner, 2022]

Obama, Barack: *A Promised Land* [Crown, 2020]

Patterson, Thomas: *How America Lost Its Mind: The Assault on Reason That's Crippling Our Democracy* [Oklahoma, 2019]

Perry, Imani: *South to America: A Journey Below the Mason-Dixon to Understand the Soul of a Nation* [Ecco, 2022]

Pinker, Steven: *Enlightenment Now: The Case for Reason, Science, Humanism, and Progress* [Penguin, 2018]

Pinker, Steven: *Rationality: What It Is, Why It Seems Scarce, Why It Matters* [Viking, 2021]

Richardson, Heather Cox: *Democracy Awakening: Notes on the State of America* [Viking, 2023]

Rindsberg, Ashley: *The Gray Lady Winked: How the* New York Times*'s Misreporting, Distortions and Fabrications Radically Alter History* [Midnight Oil Publishers, 2021]

Risen, James: *Pay Any Price: Greed, Power, and Endless War* [Mariner Books, 2015]

Rothstein, Richard: *The Color of Law: A Forgotten History of How Our Government Segregated America* [Norton, 2018]

Rufo, Christopher F.: *America's Cultural Revolution: How the Radical Left Conquered Everything* [Broadside Books, 2023]

Rumsfeld, Donald: *Known and Unknown: A Memoir* [Sentinel, 2012]

Silver, Nate: *The Signal and the Noise: Why So Many Predictions Fail—but Some Don't* [Penguin, 2012]

Snyder, Timothy: *On Tyranny: Twenty Lessons from the Twentieth Century* [Crown, 2017]

Sowell, Thomas: *Economic Facts and Fallacies* [Basic Books, 2011]

Stevenson, Bryan: *Just Mercy: A Story of Justice and Redemption* [One World, 2014]

Suskind, Ron: *The Price of Loyalty: George W. Bush, the White House, and the Education of Paul O'Neill* [Simon & Schuster, 2004]

Tavris, Carol; Aronson, Elliot: *Mistakes Were Made (But Not by Me): Why We Justify Foolish Beliefs, Bad Decisions, and Hurtful Acts* [Harvest Books, 2008]

Vance, J. D.: *Hillbilly Elegy: A Memoir of a Family and Culture in Crisis* [Harper, 2016]

Wegman, Jesse: *Let the People Pick the President: The Case for Abolishing the Electoral College* [St. Martin's Press, 2020]

Will, George F.: *The Leveling Wind: Politics, the Culture, and Other News* [Penguin, 1995]

Williams, Joan C.: *White Working Class: Overcoming Class Cluelessness in America* [Harvard Business Review Press, 2017]

Woodward, Bob; Costa, Robert: *Peril* [Simon & Schuster, 2021]

Woodward, Bob: *Rage* [Simon & Schuster, 2020]

Yoo, John: *War by Other Means: An Insider's Account of the War on Terror* [Atlantic Monthly Press, 2006]

Zeihan, Peter: *Disunited Nations: The Scramble for Power in an Ungoverned World* [Harper Business, 2020]

Zeihan, Peter: *The End of the World Is Just the Beginning: Mapping the Collapse of Globalization* [Harper Business, 2022]

Zinn, Howard: *A People's History of the United States* [Harper, 1980]